How to Draw Cars, Trucks, Planes, and Other things

How to Draw Vehicles Books for Kids

by DS Creation

Published by:

DS Creation

©Copyright 2019 – DS Creation

ISBN: 9798603140988

ALL RIGHTS RESERVED. No part of this publication may be reproduced or transmitted in any form whatsoever, electronic, or mechanical, including photocopying, recording, or by any informational storage or retrieval system without express written, dated and signed permission from the author.

Table of Contents

Draw a Plane........................1

Draw a Plane for Kids.......8

Draw an El Camino.........15

Draw Easy Truck.............24

Draw the Hennessey Venom GT 30

Draw a Plane

Step-1

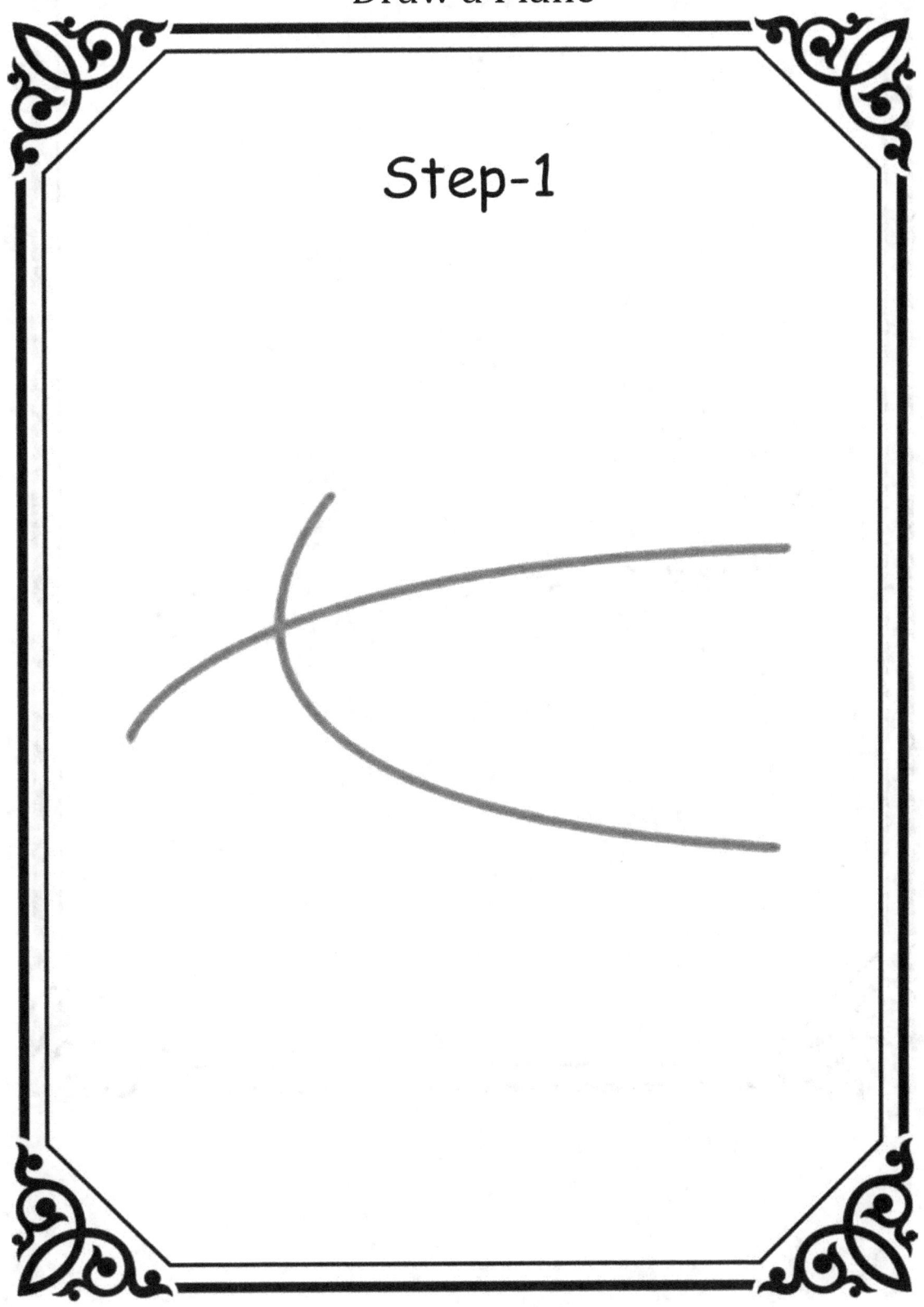

Step-2

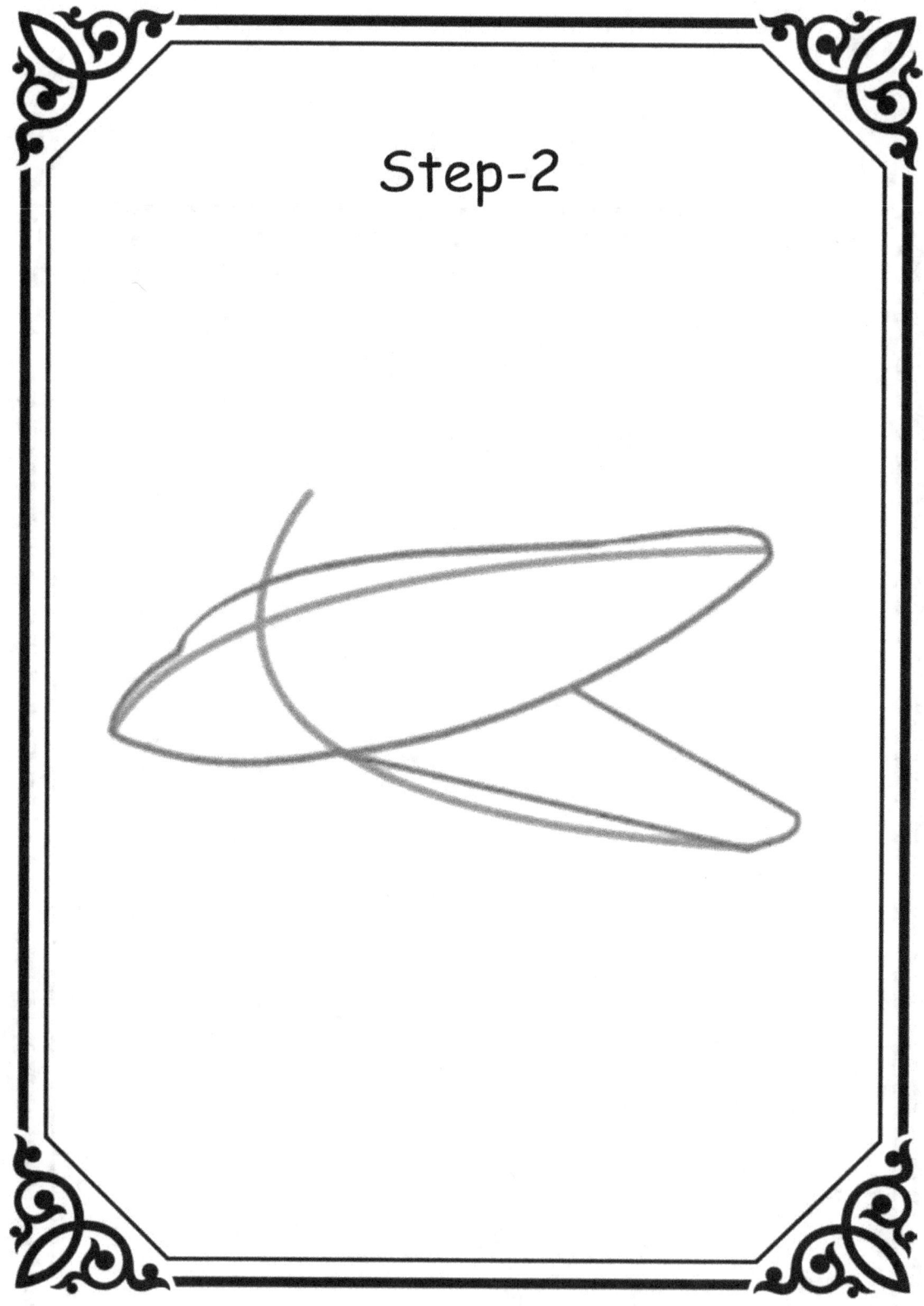

Step-3

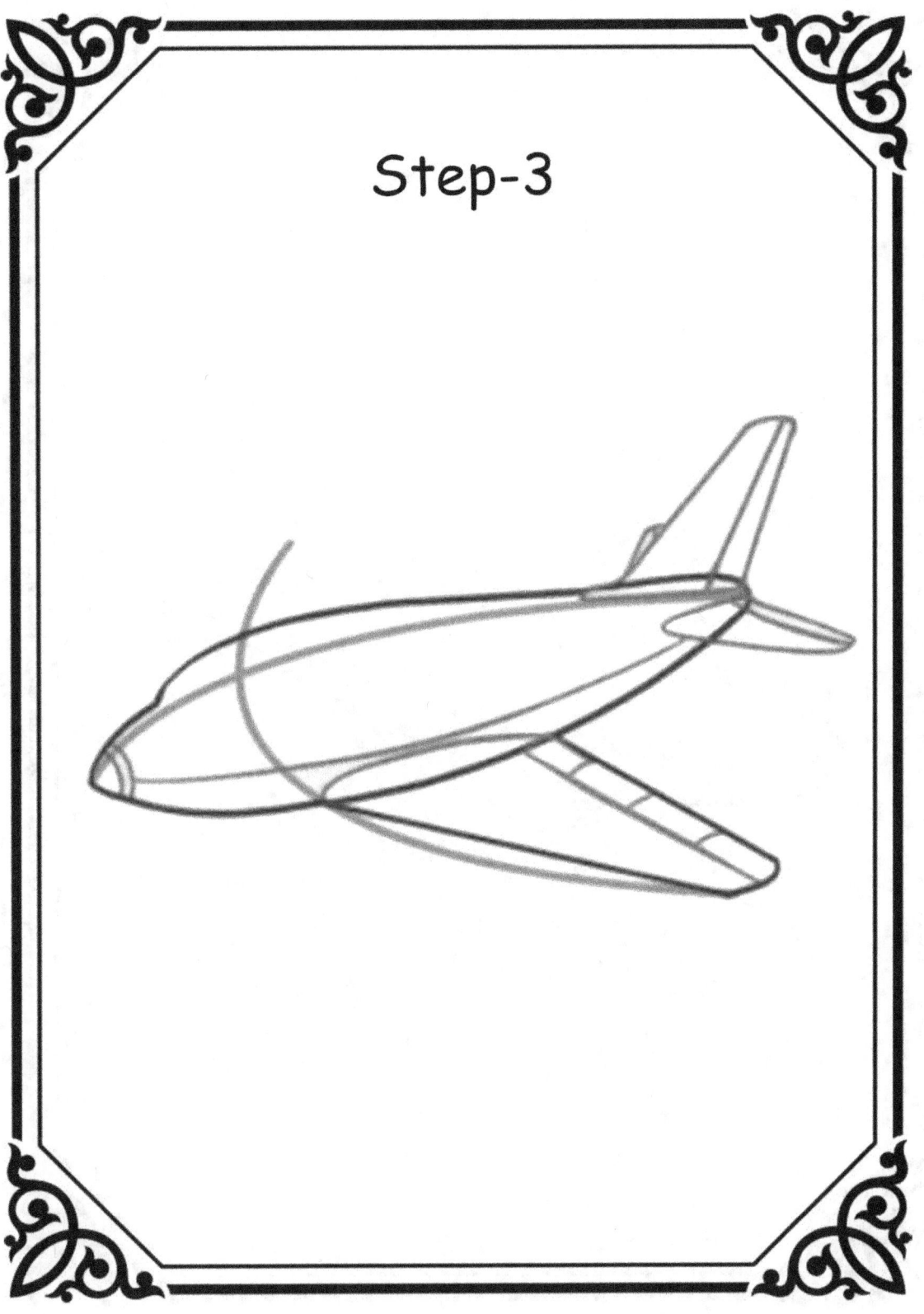

Step-4

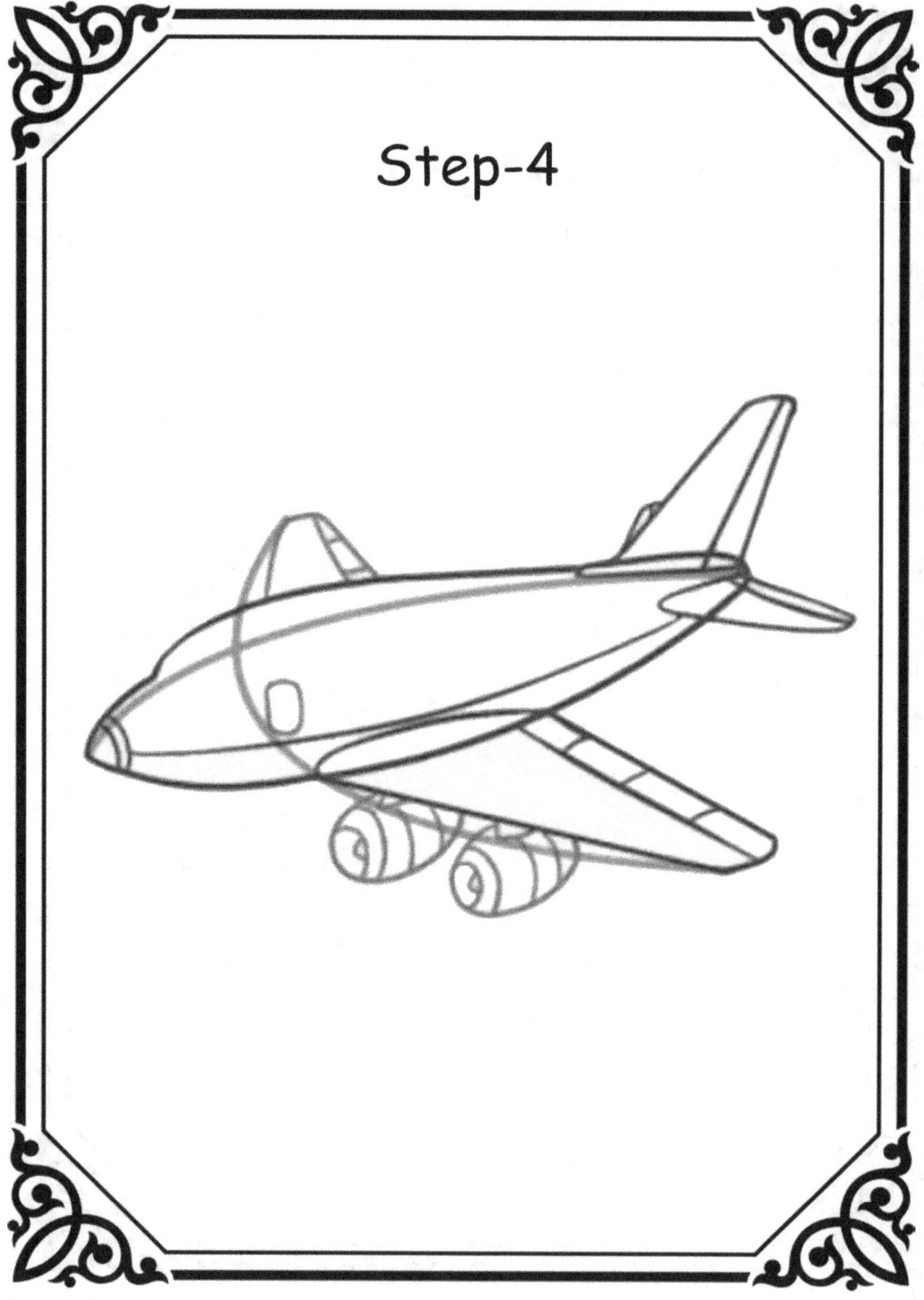

Step-5

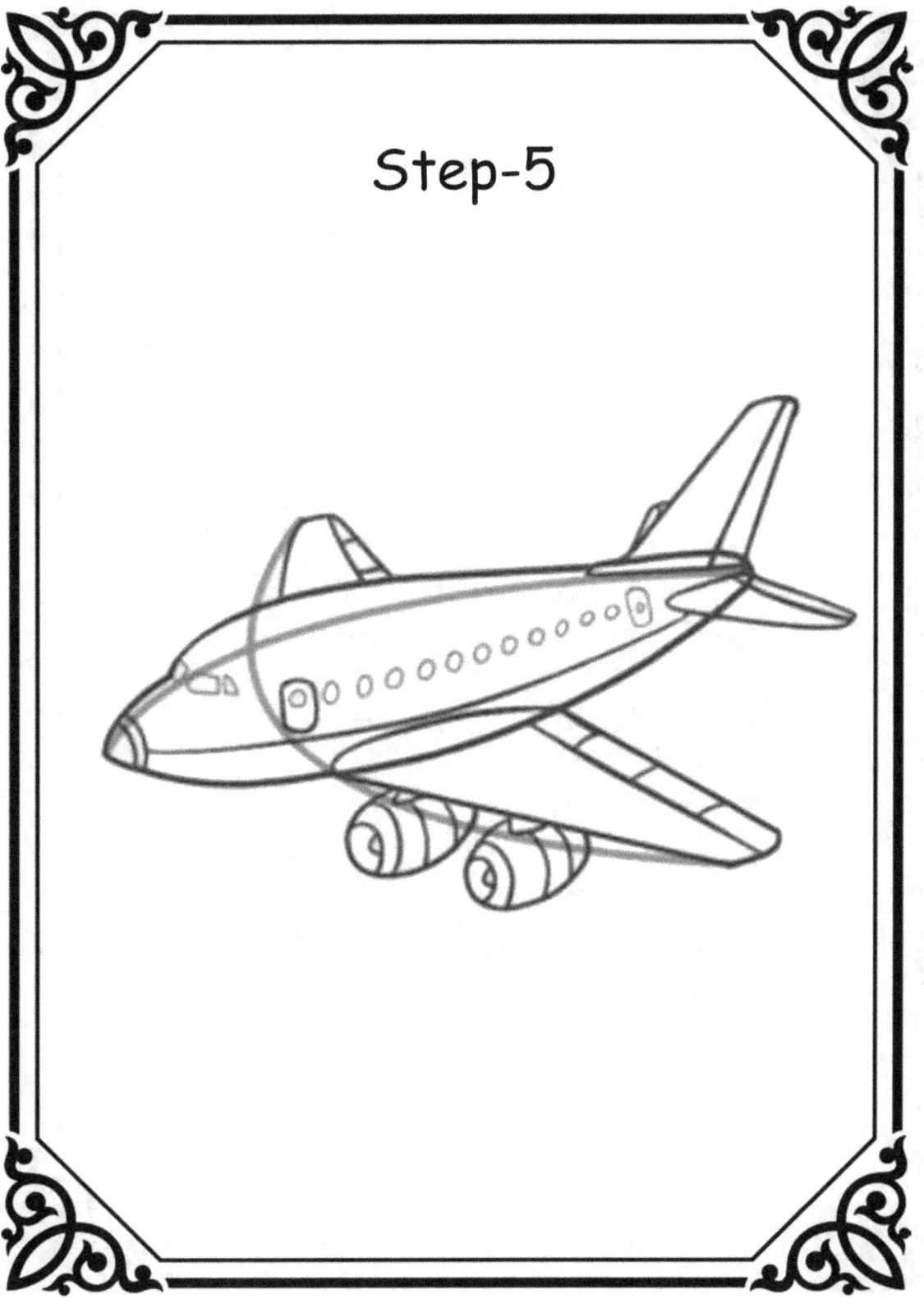

Step-6

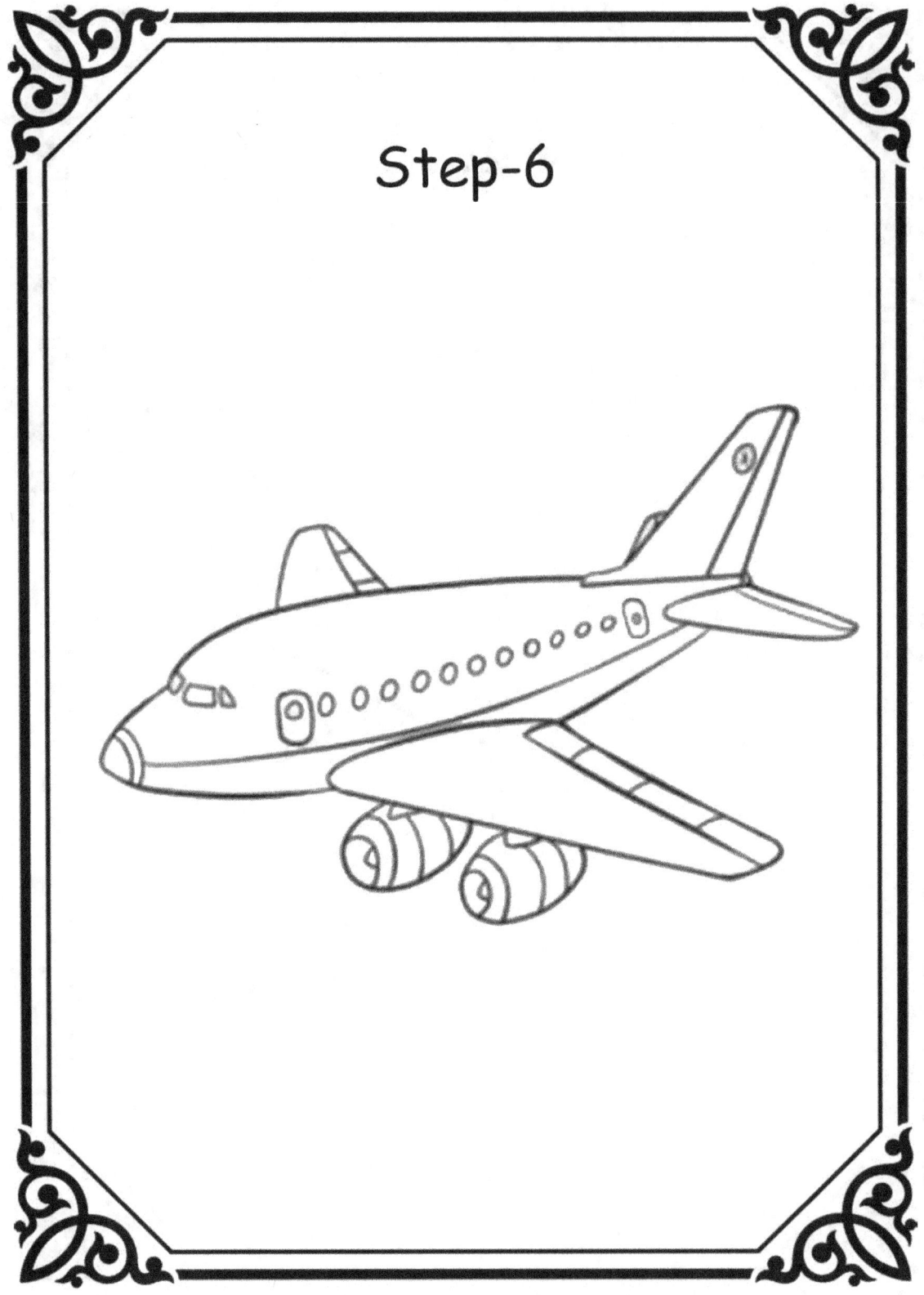

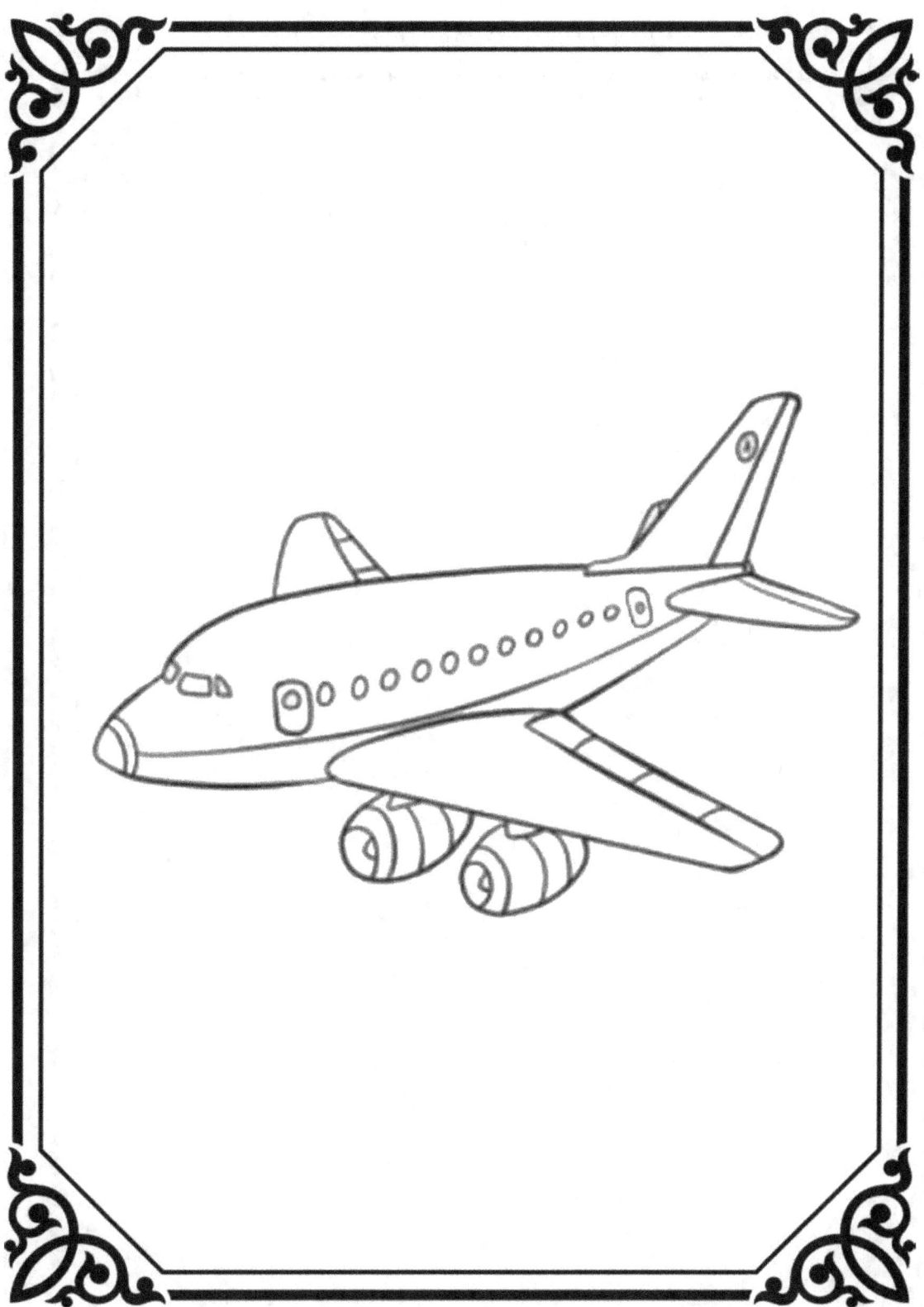

Draw a Plane for Kids

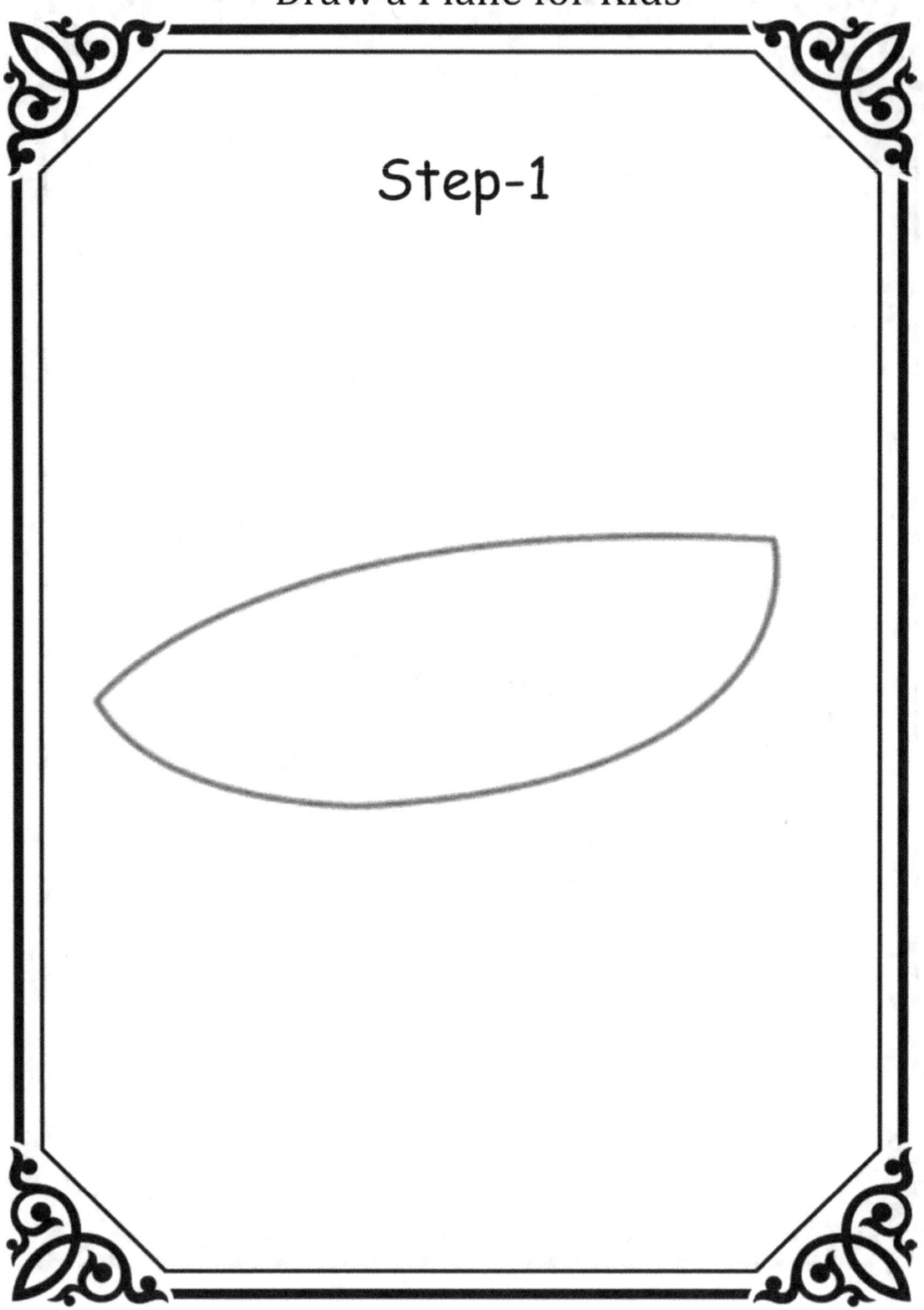

Step-2

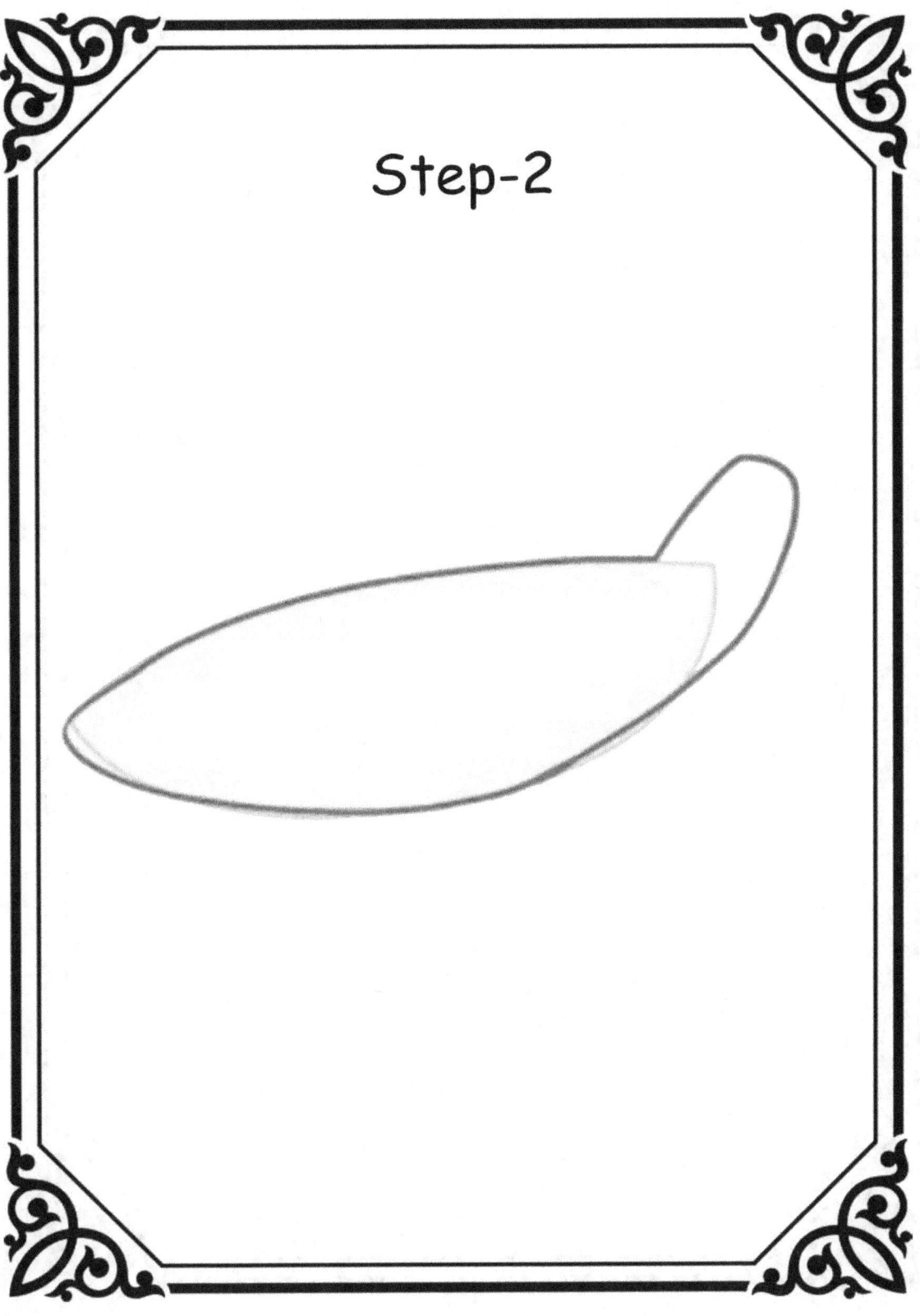

Step-3

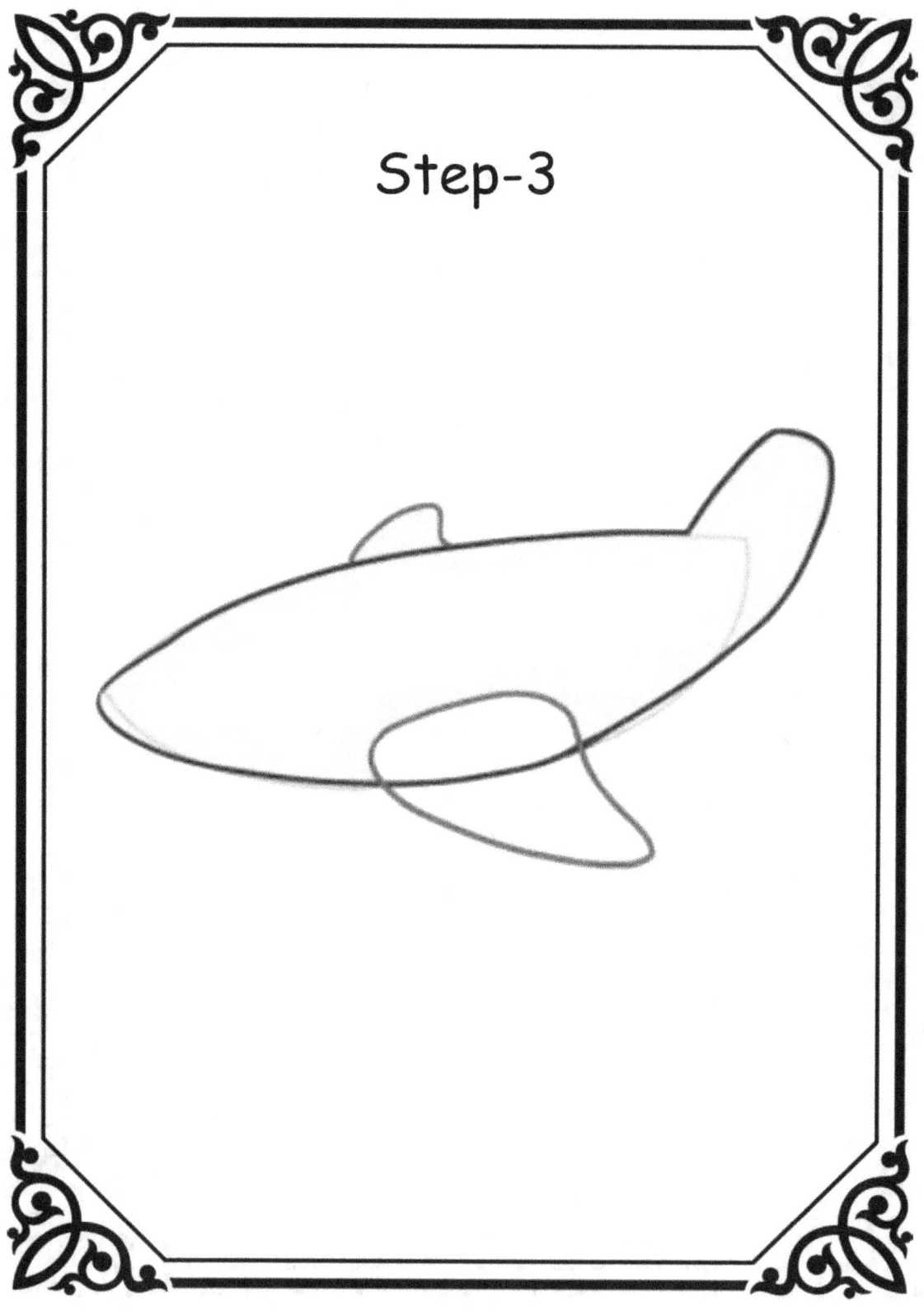

Step-4

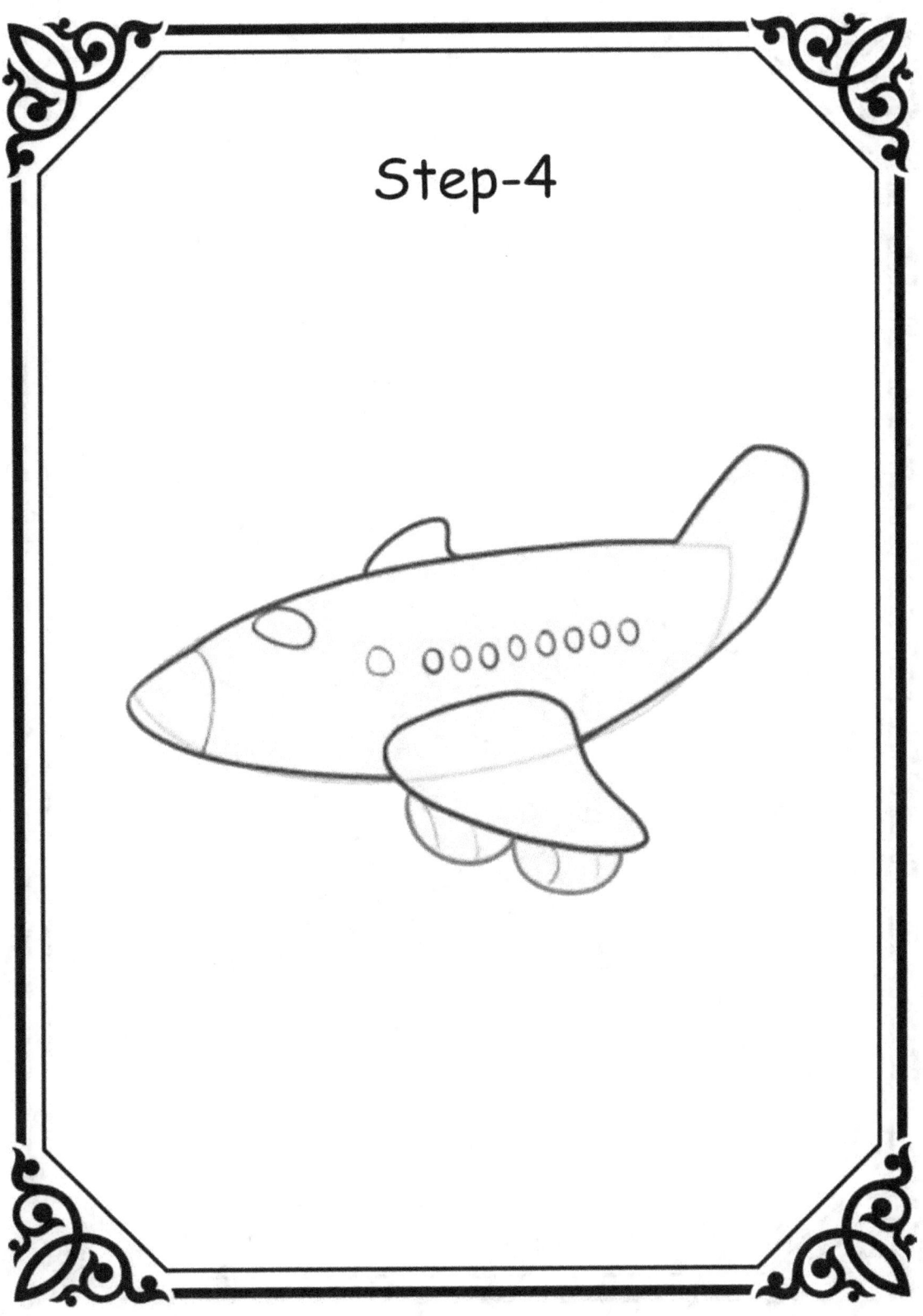

Step-5

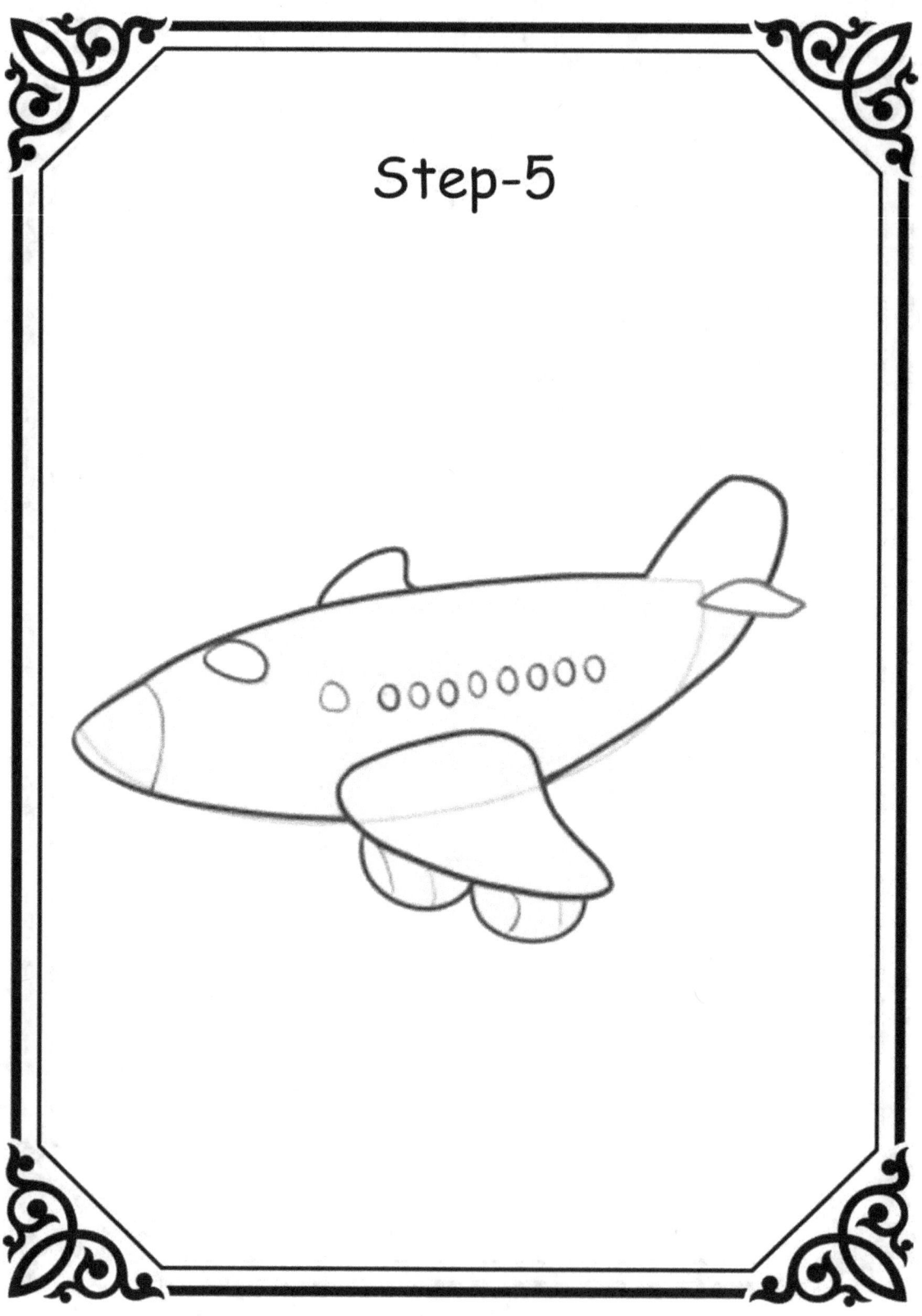

Step-6

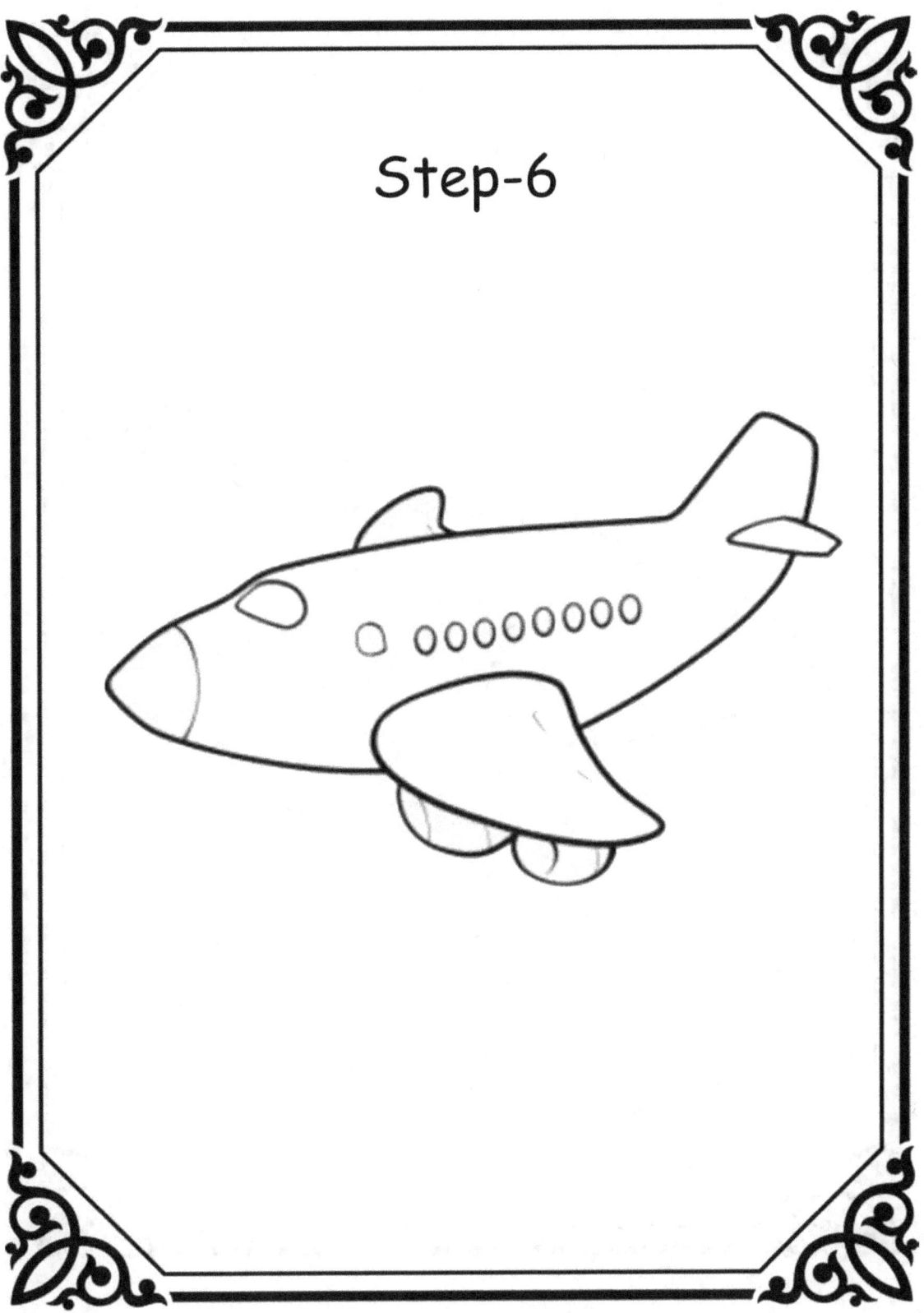

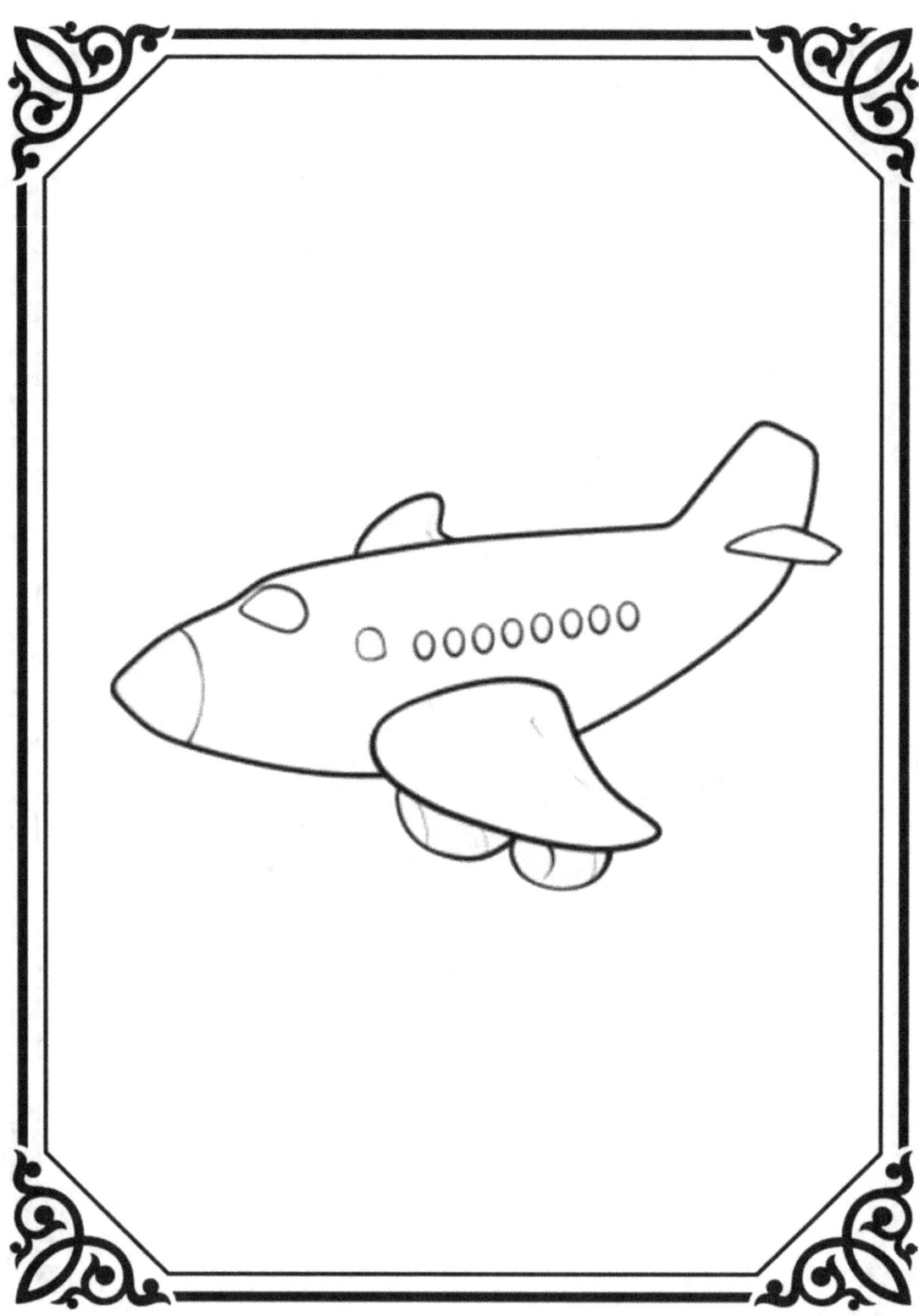

Draw an El Camino

Step-1

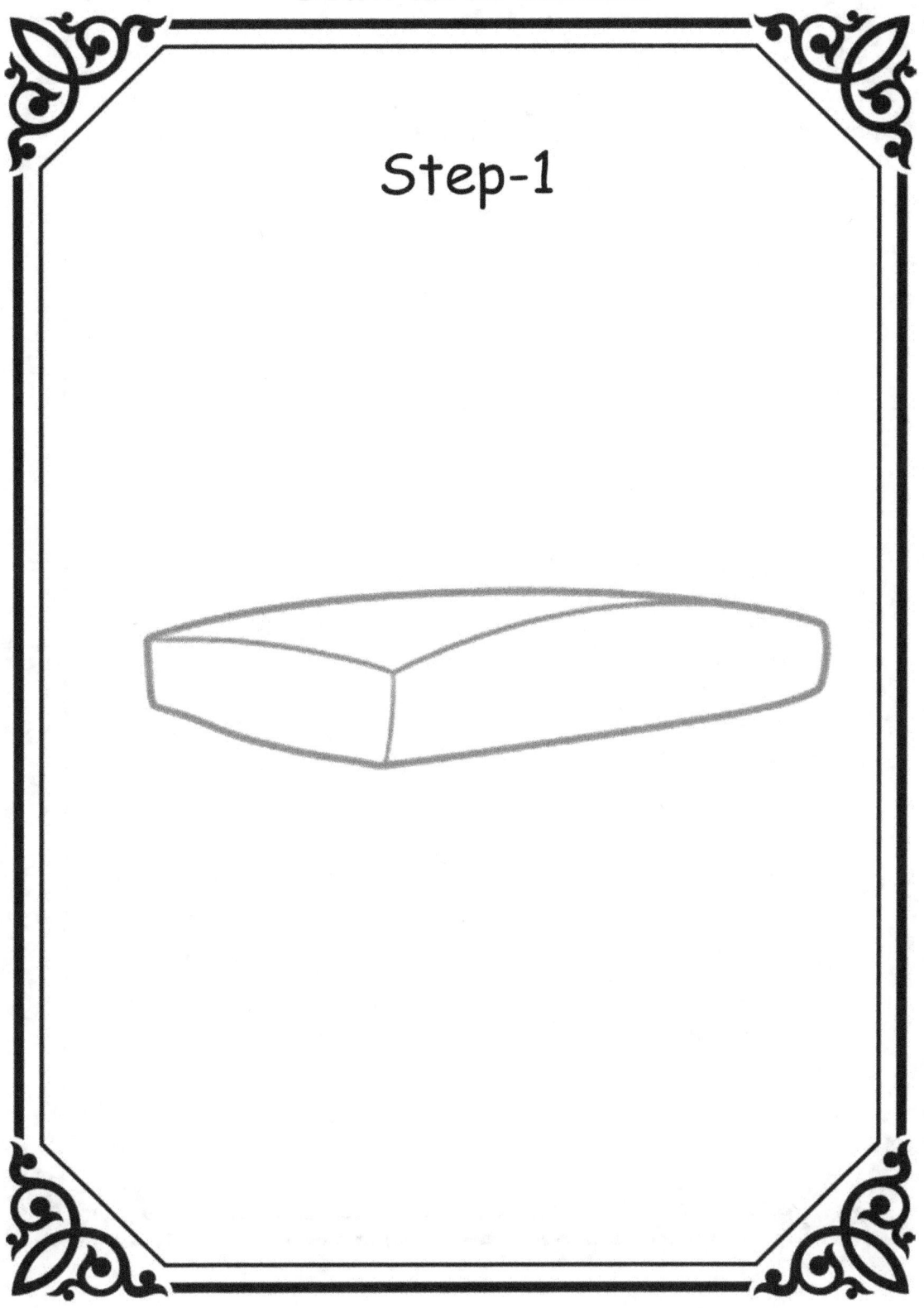

Step-2

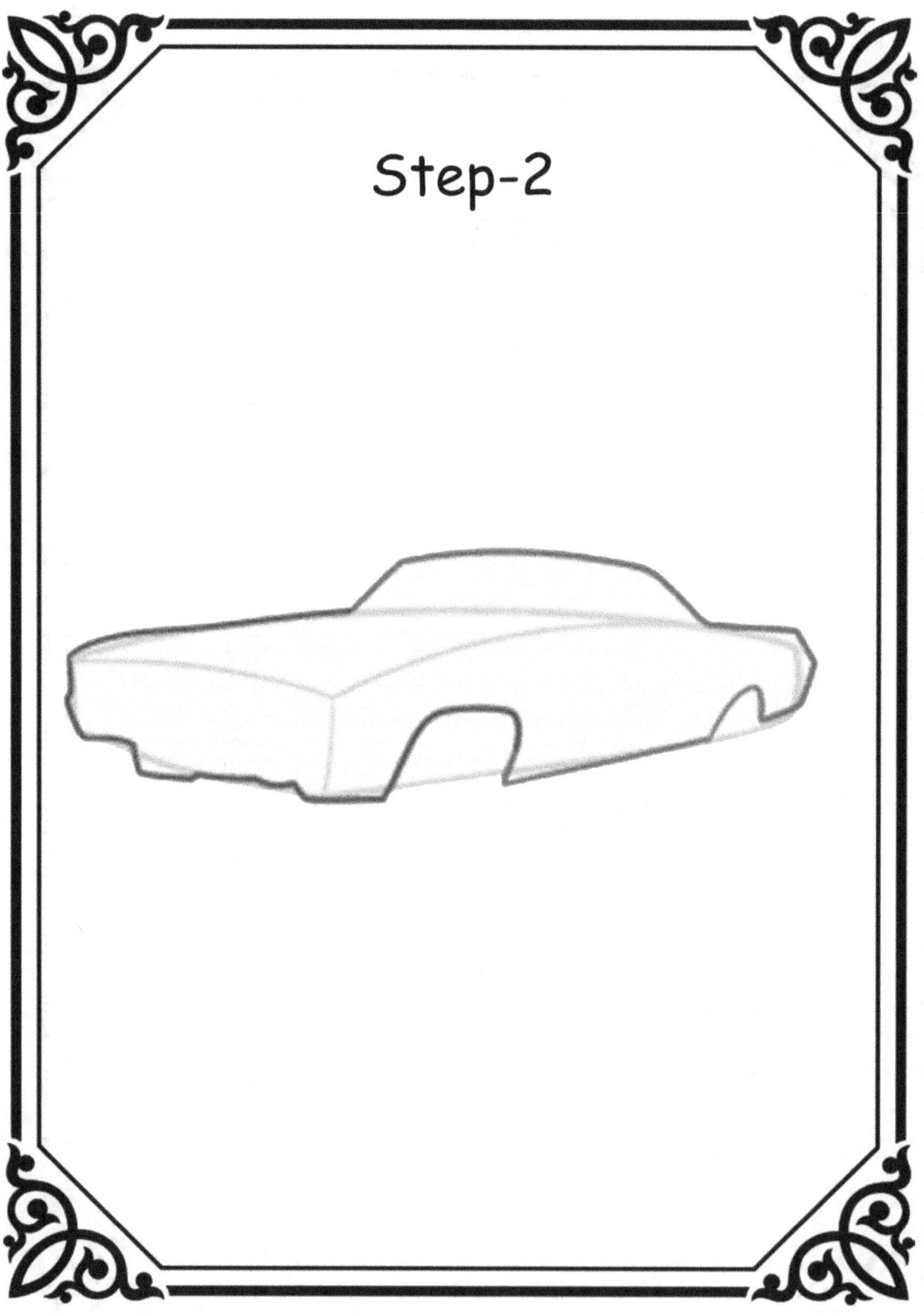

Step-3

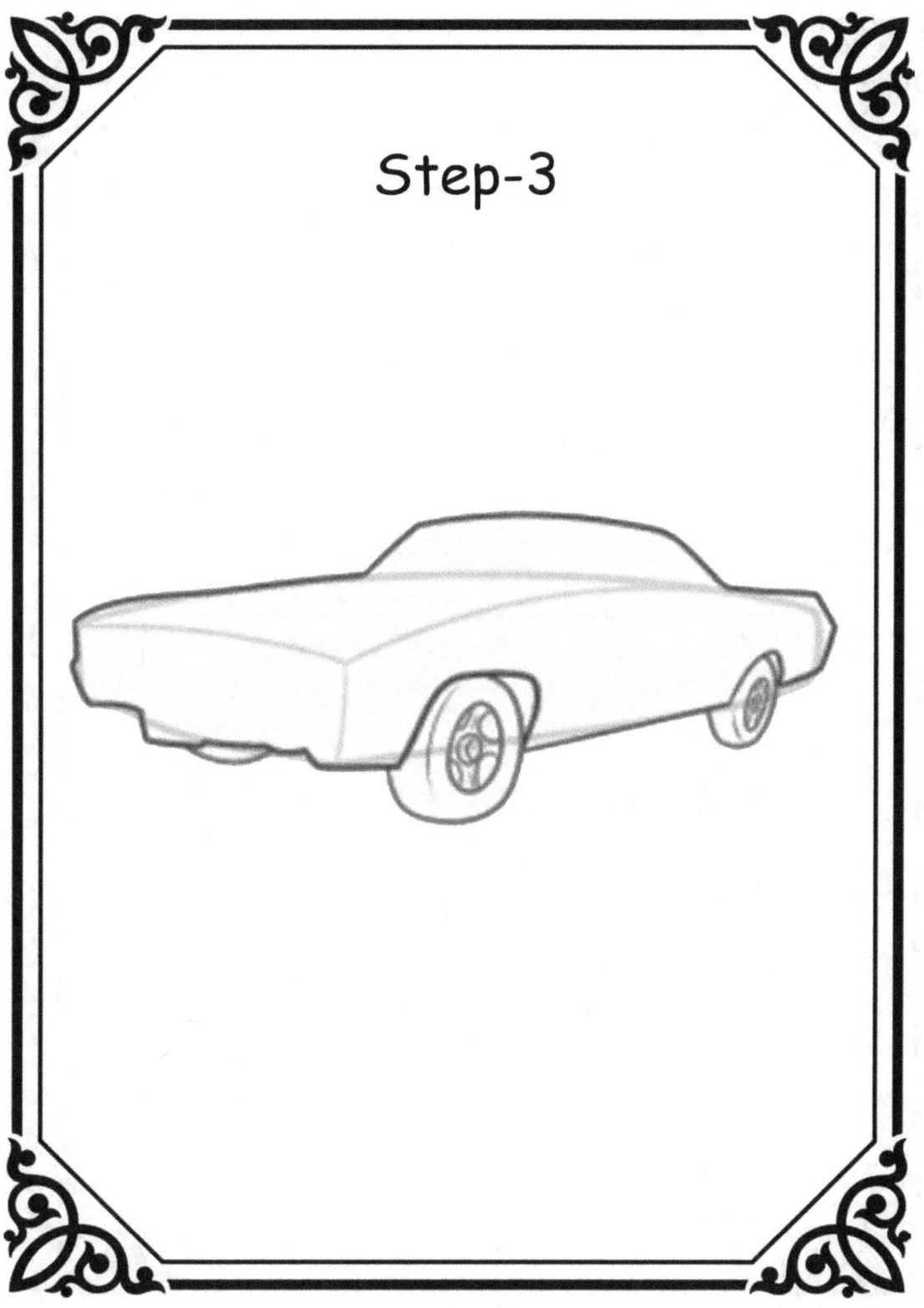

Step-4

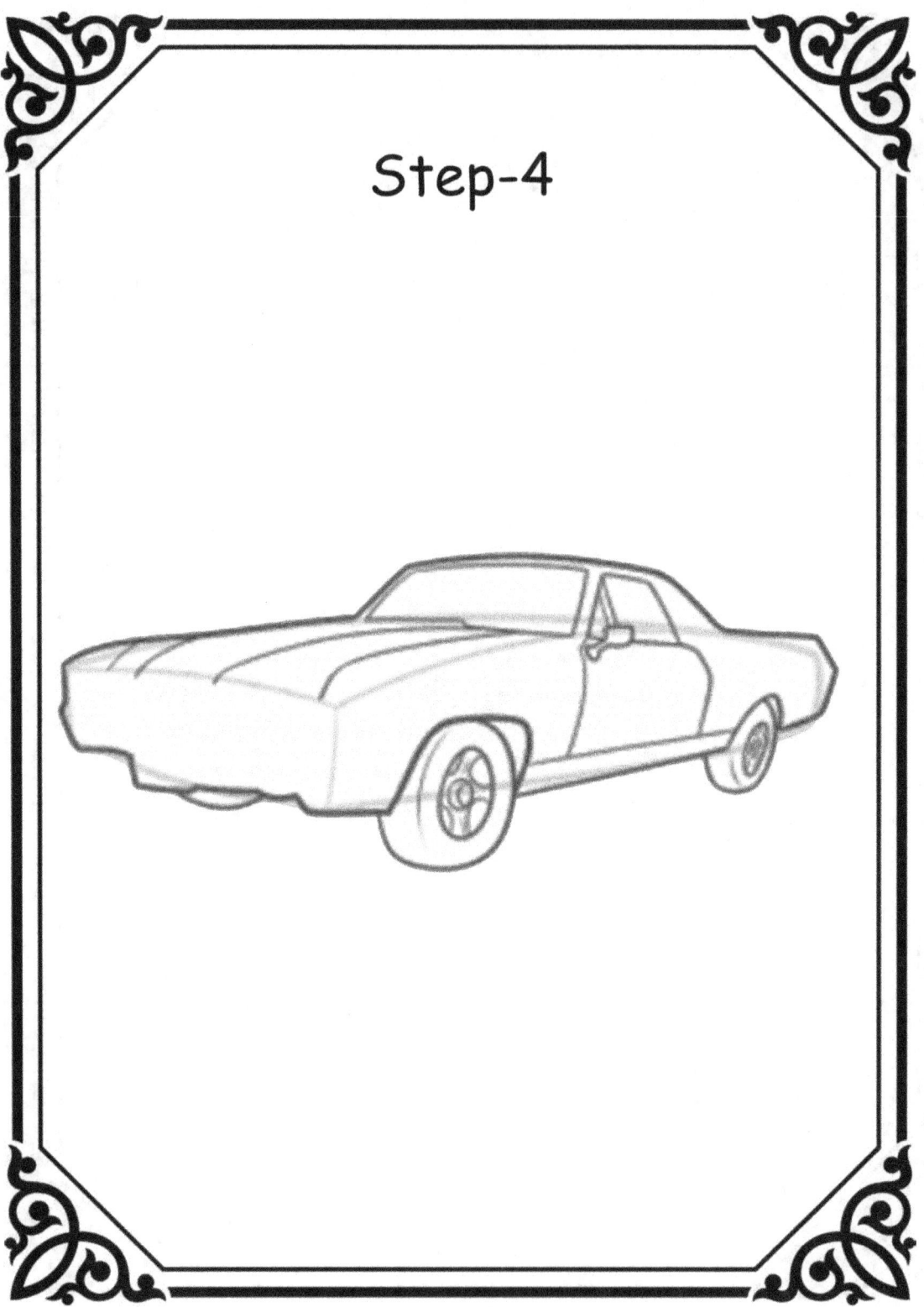

Step-5

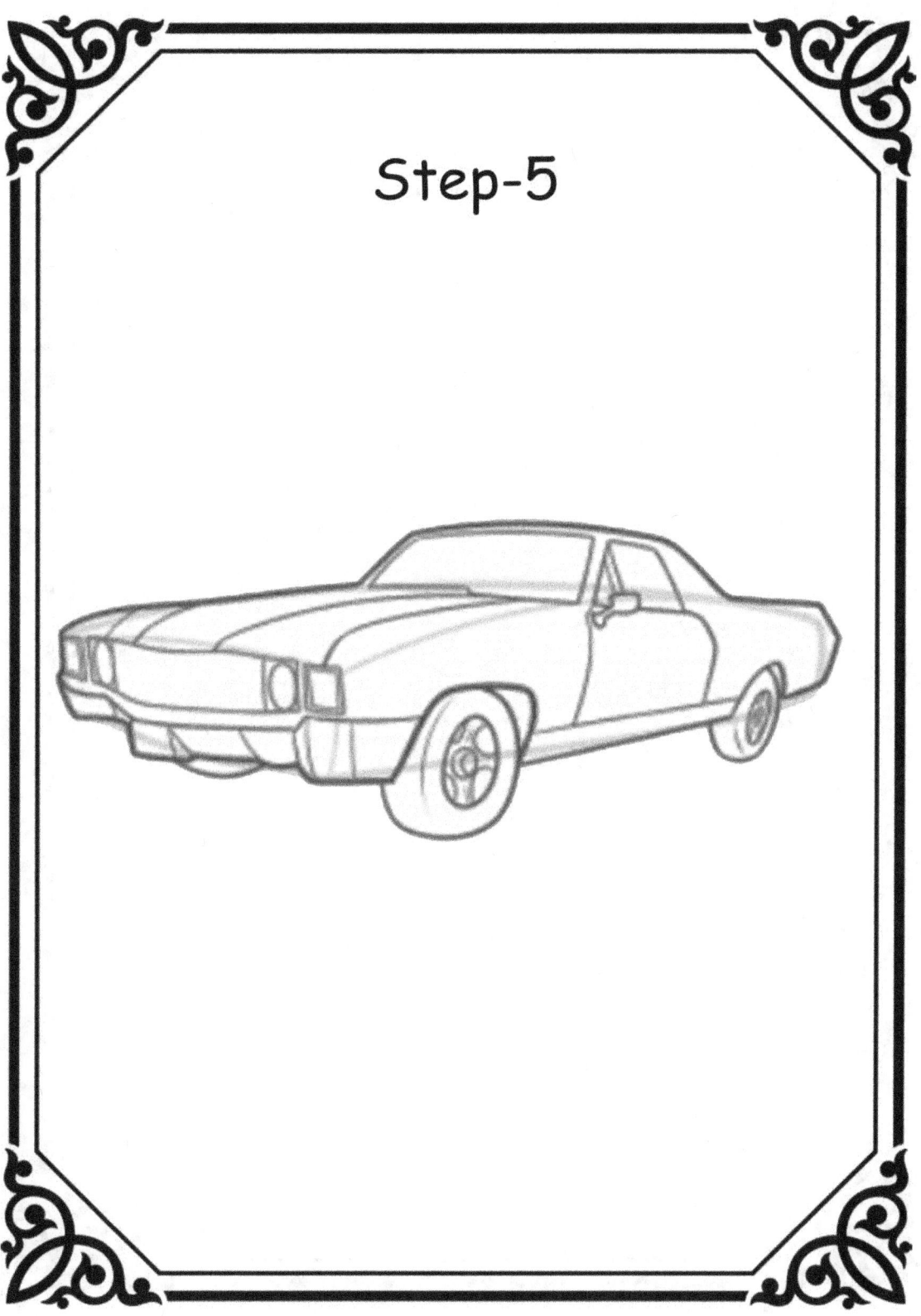

Step-6

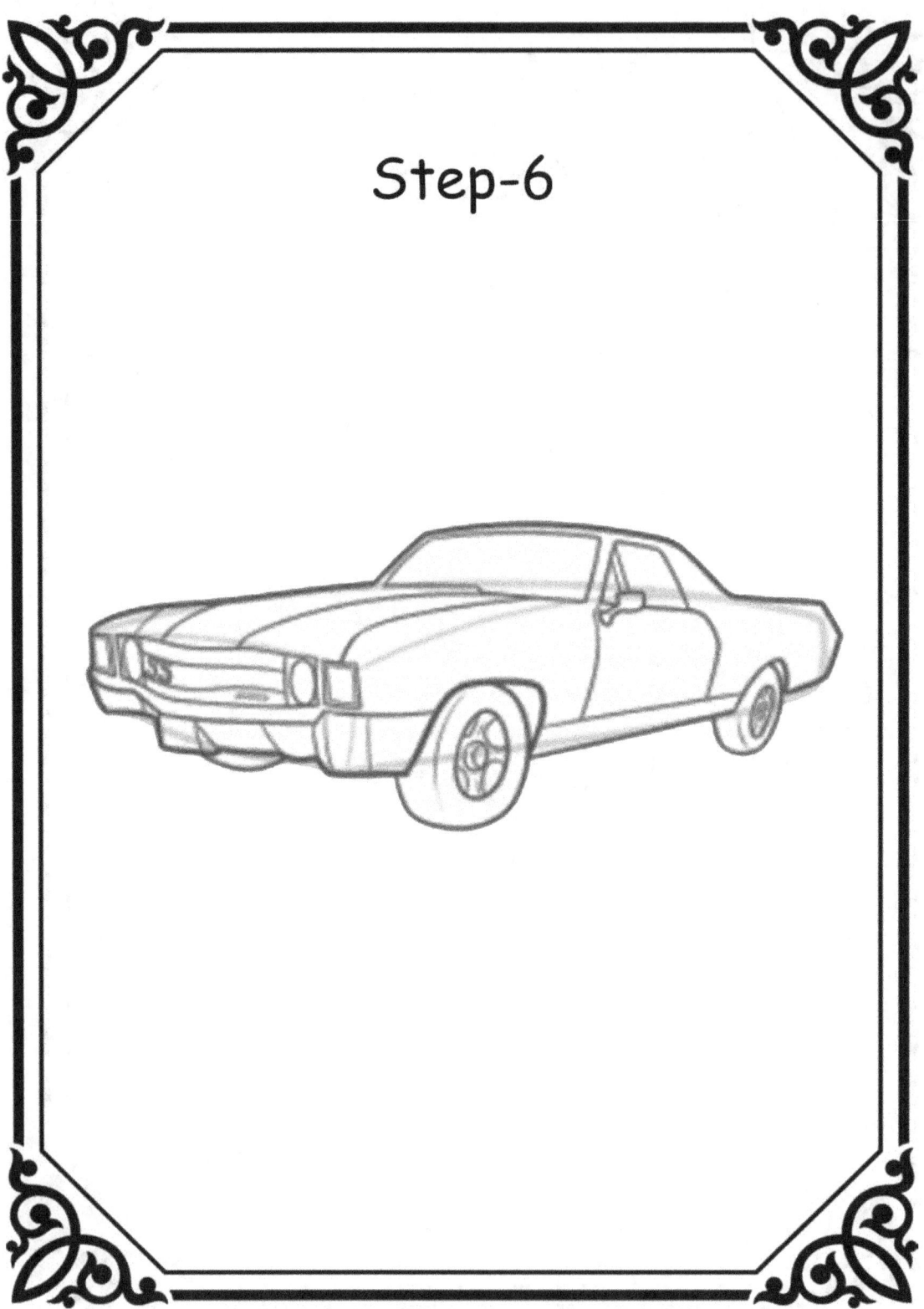

Step-7

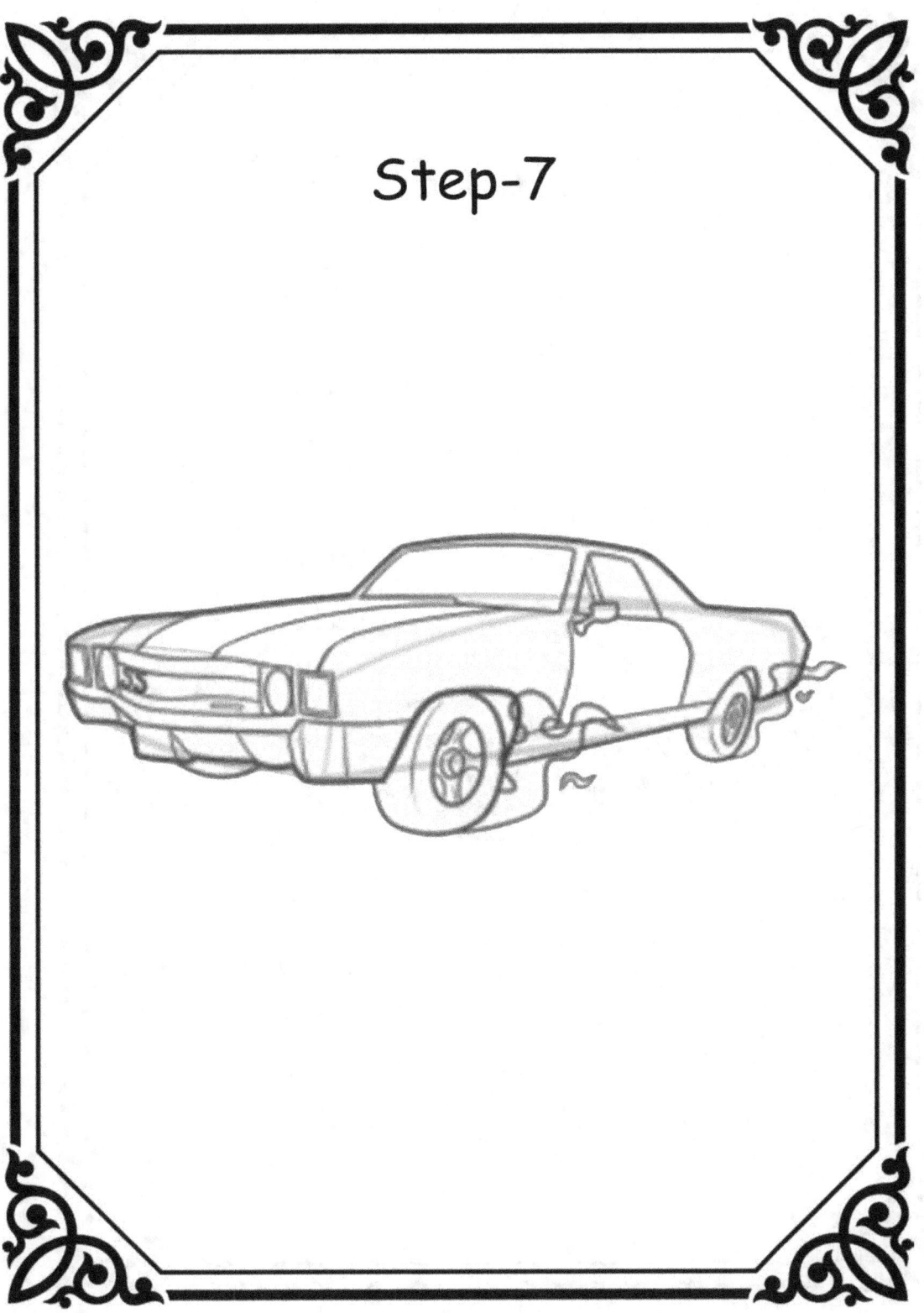

Step-8

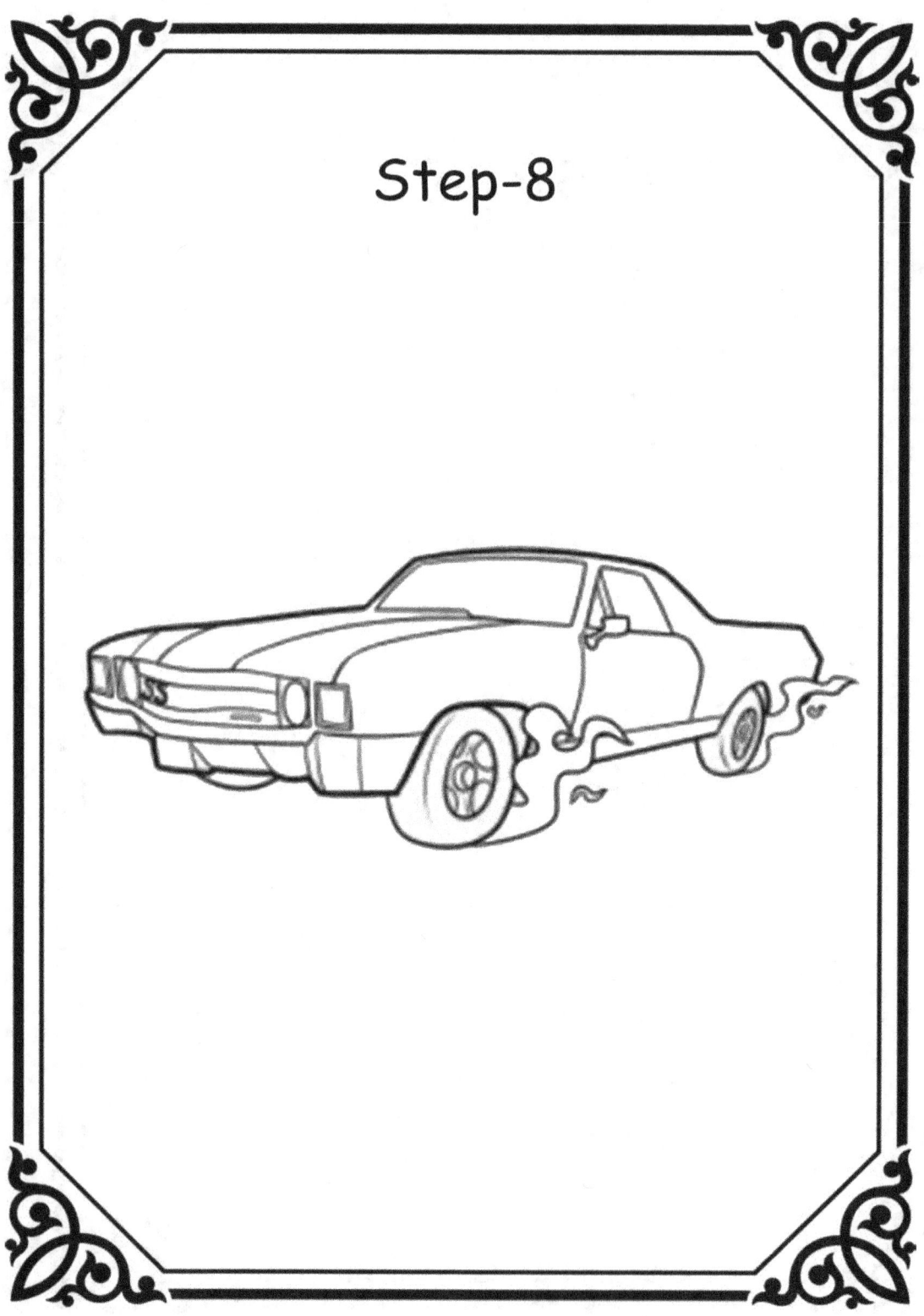

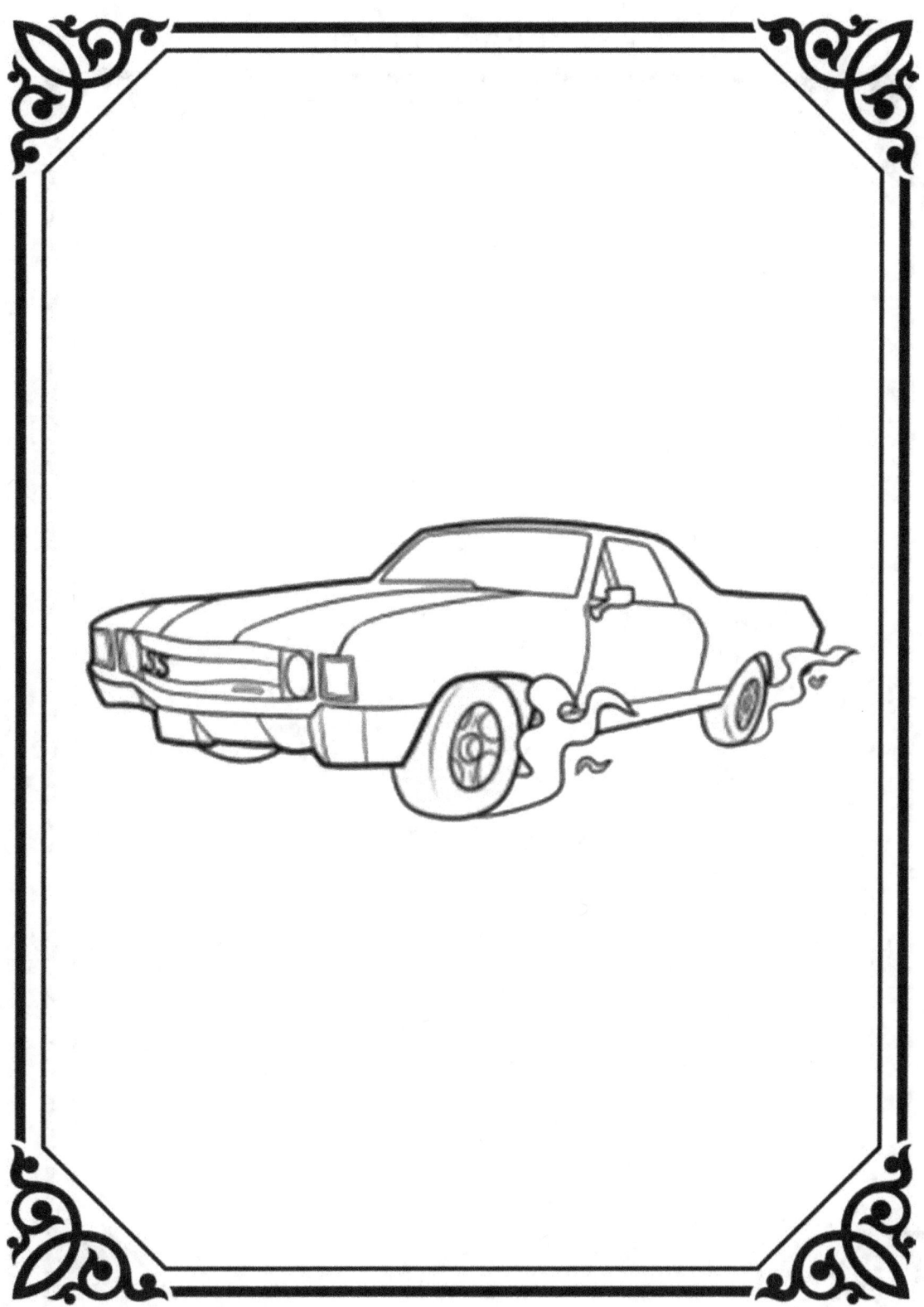

Draw Easy Truck

Step-1

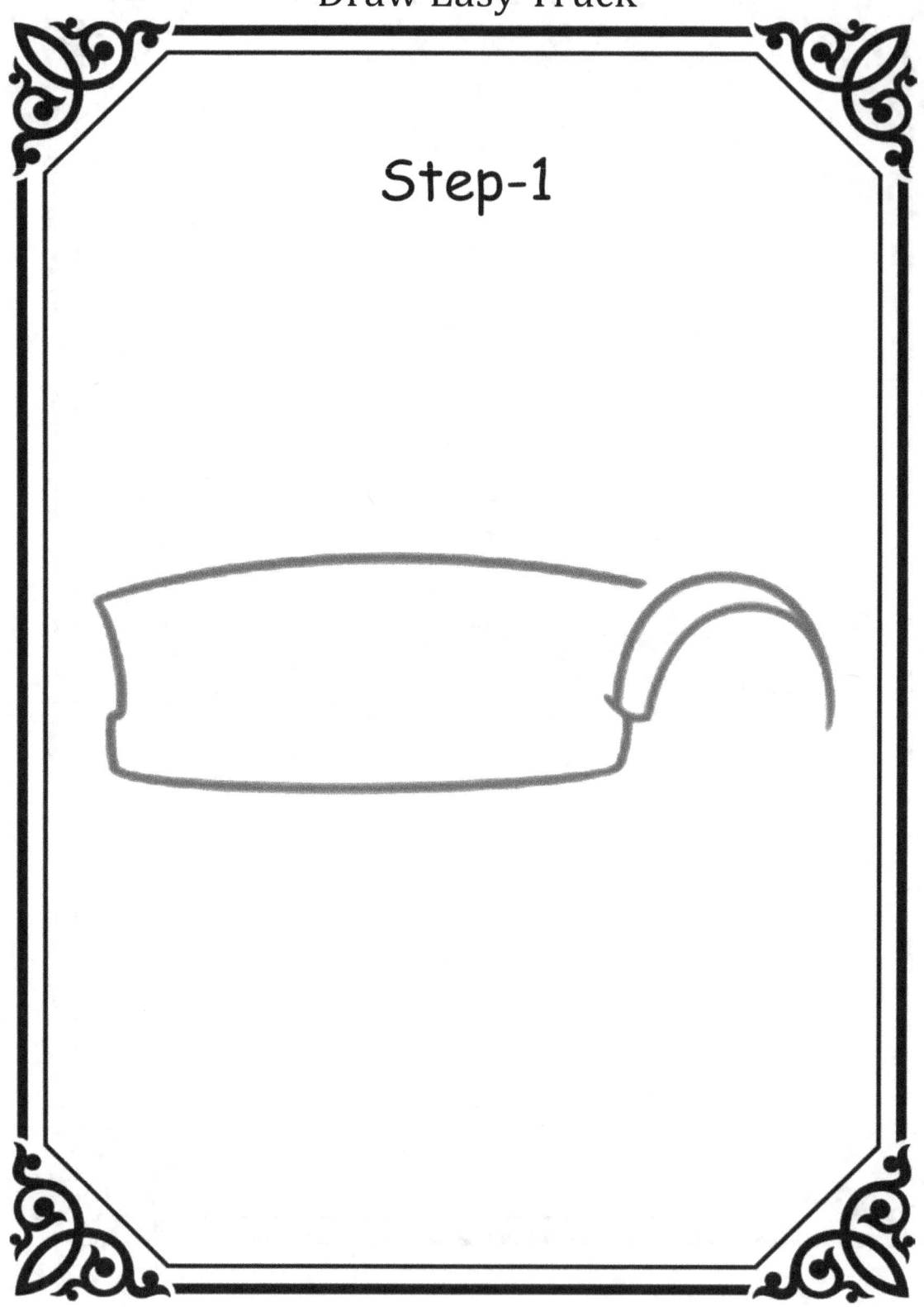

Step-2

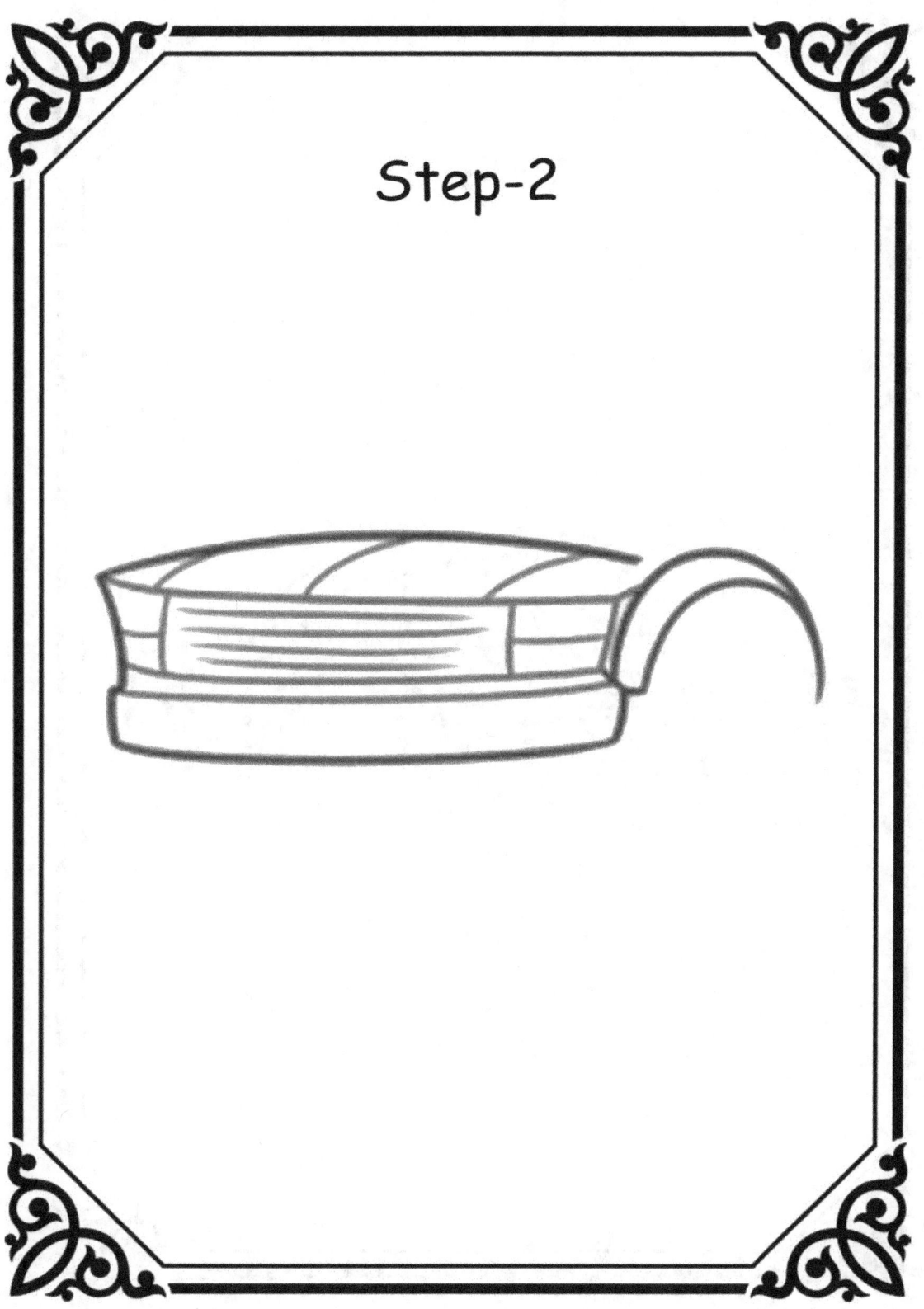

Step-3

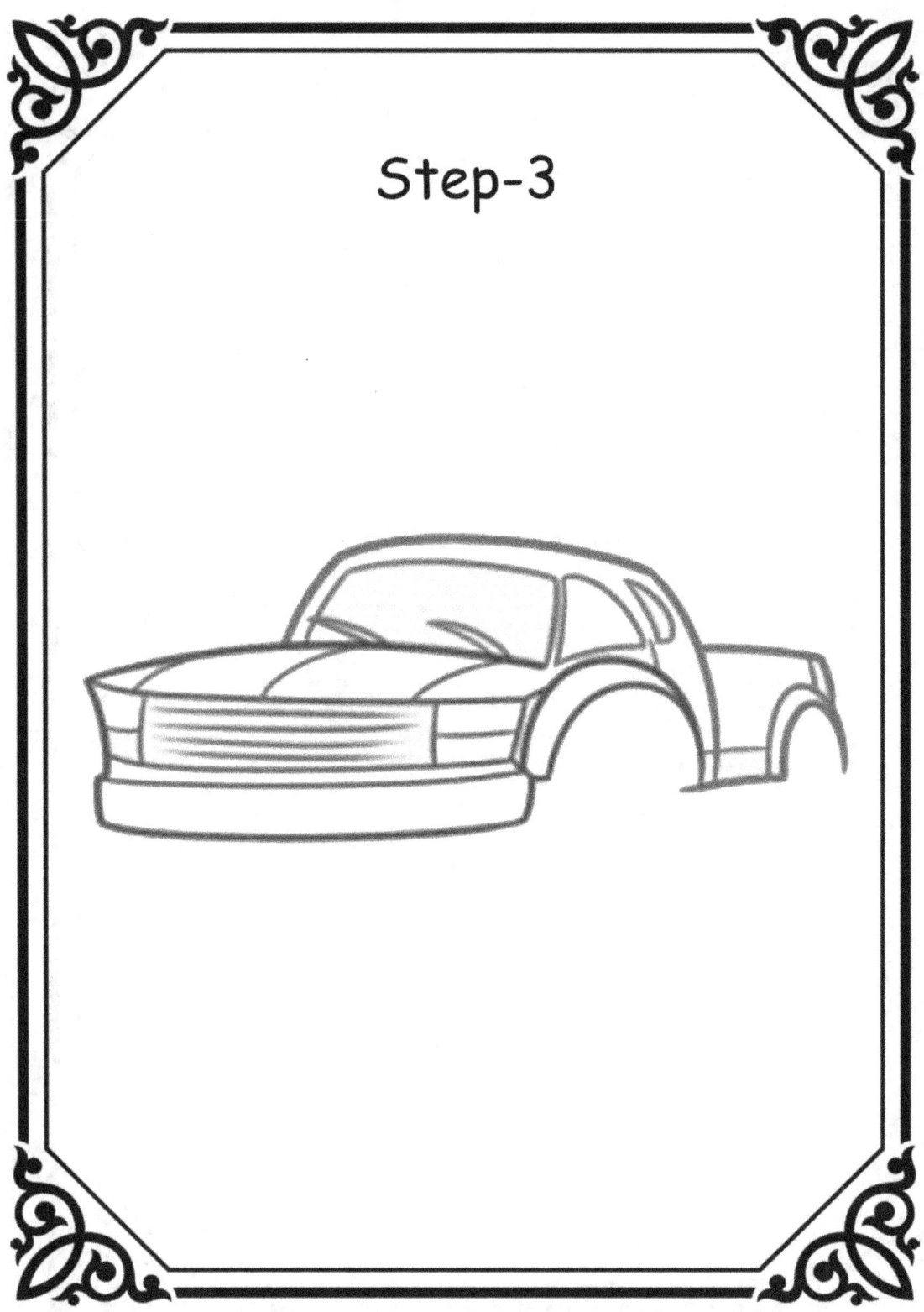

Step-4

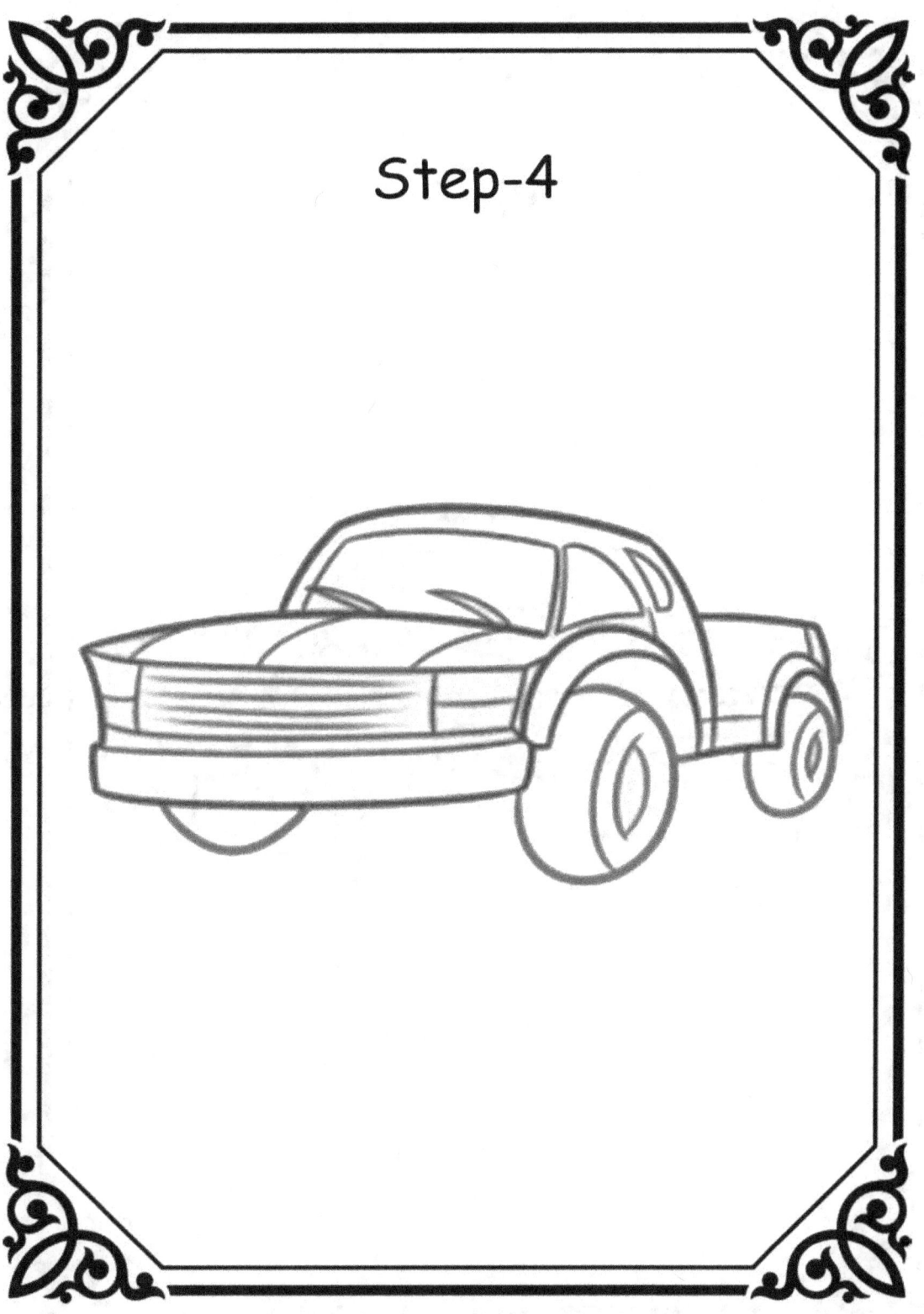

Step-5

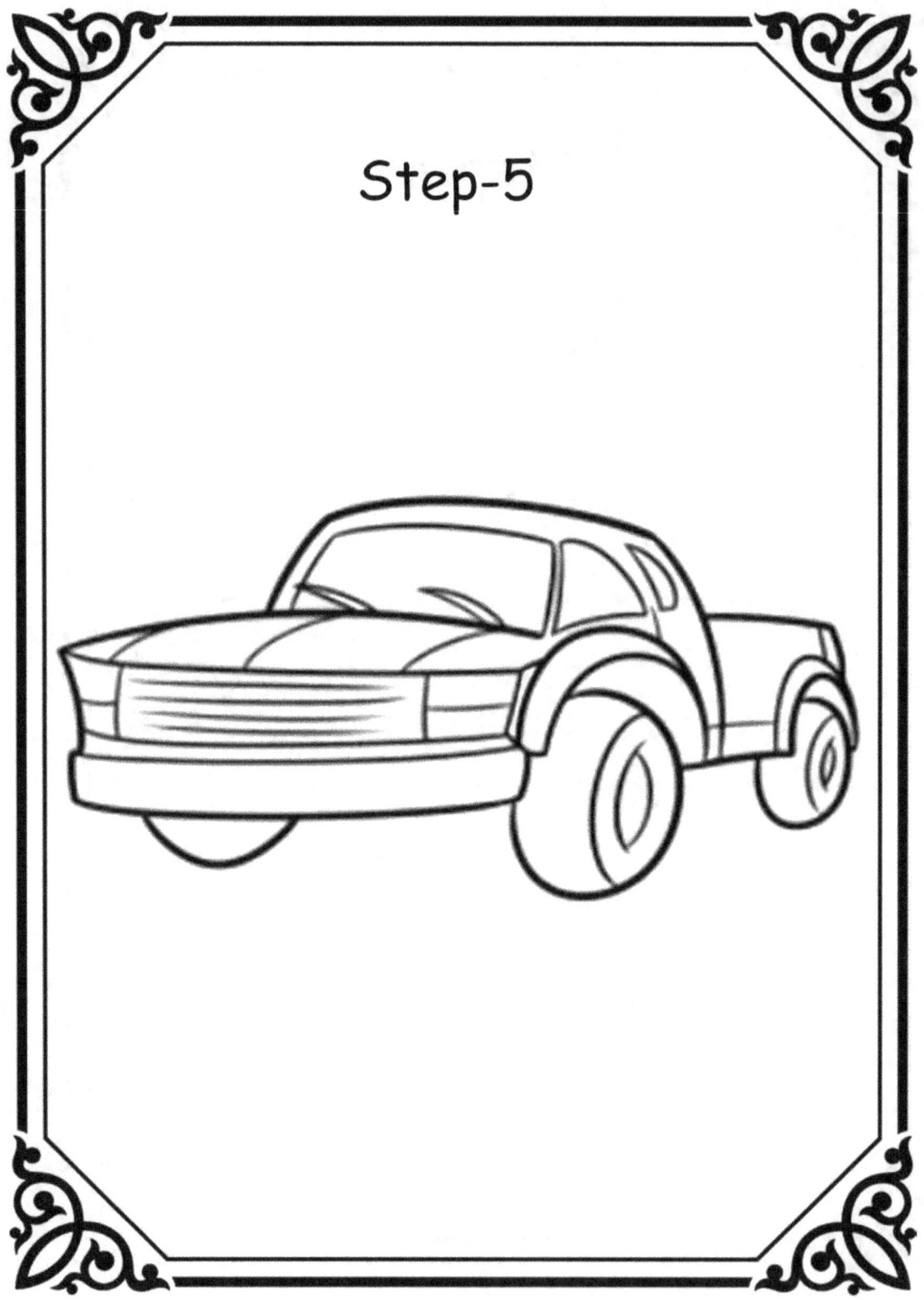

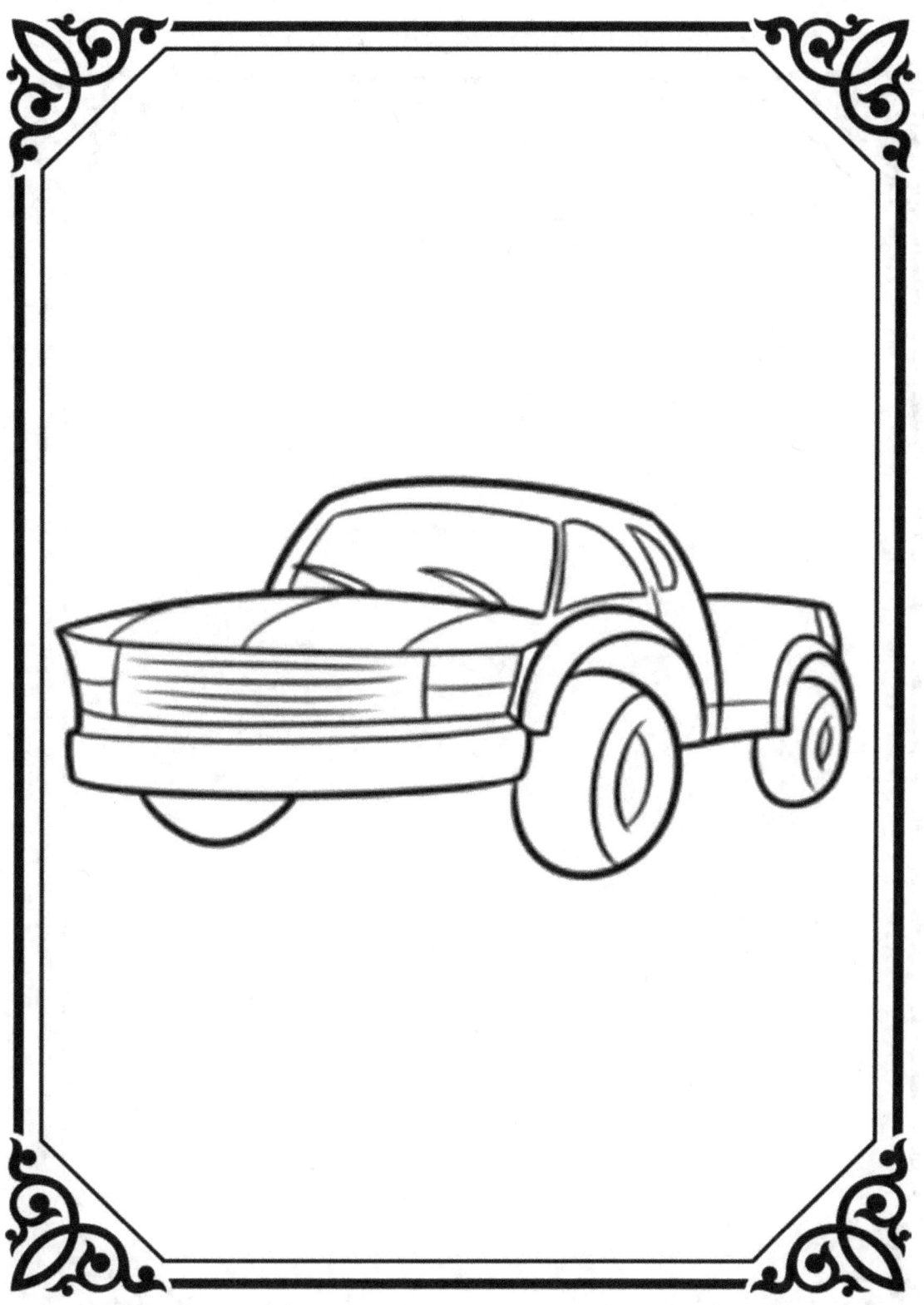

Draw the Hennessey Venom GT

Step-1

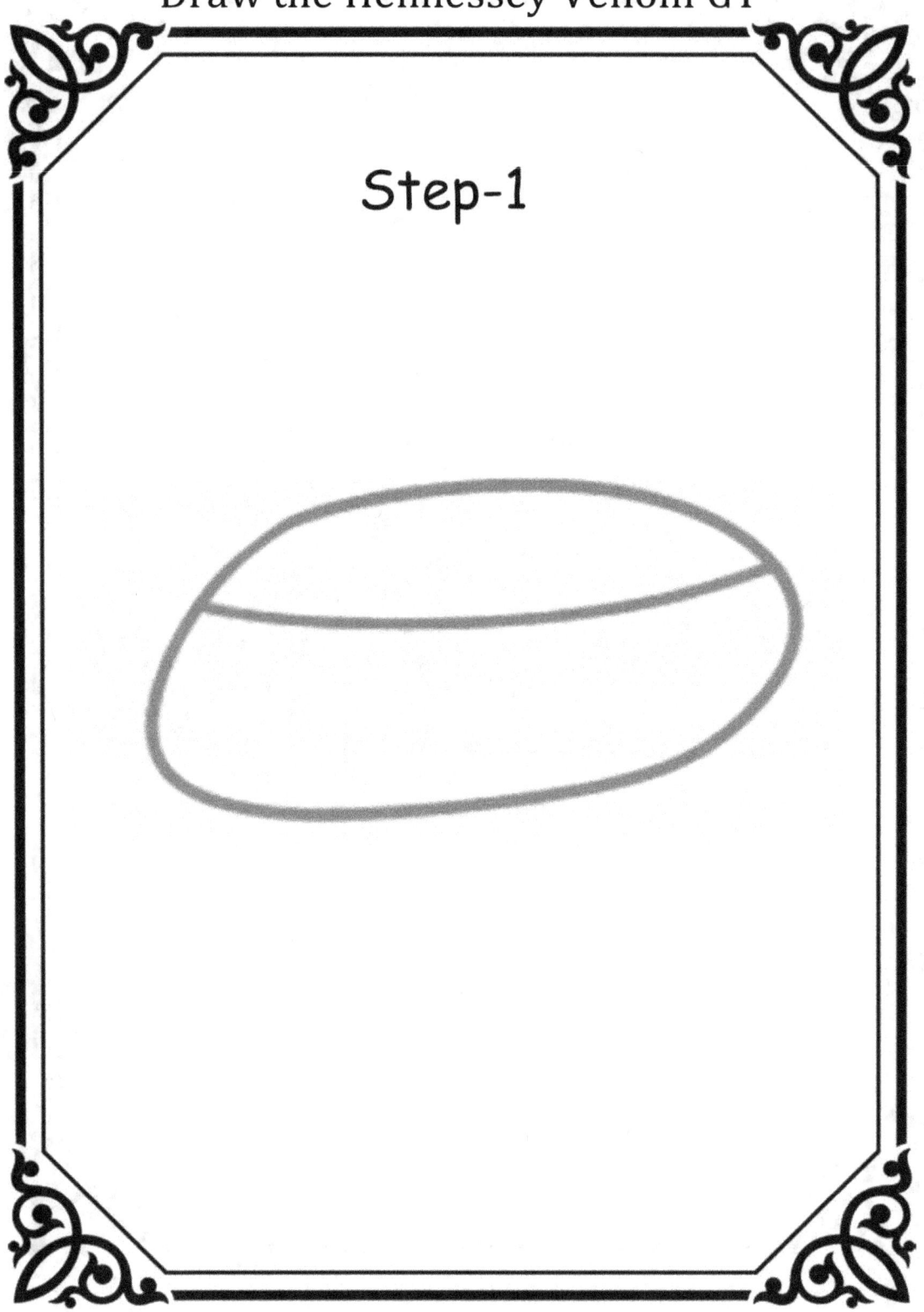

Step-2

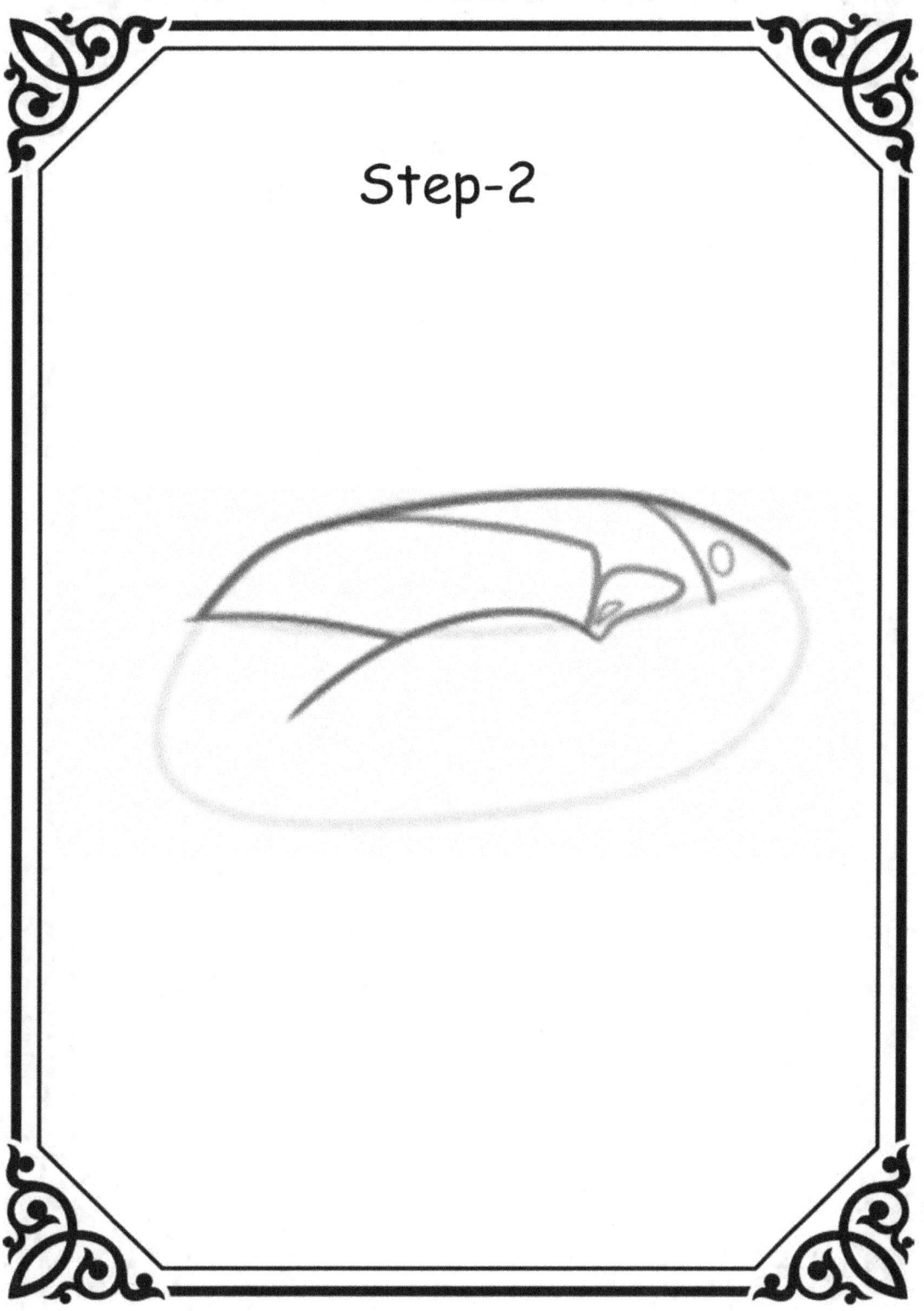

Step-3

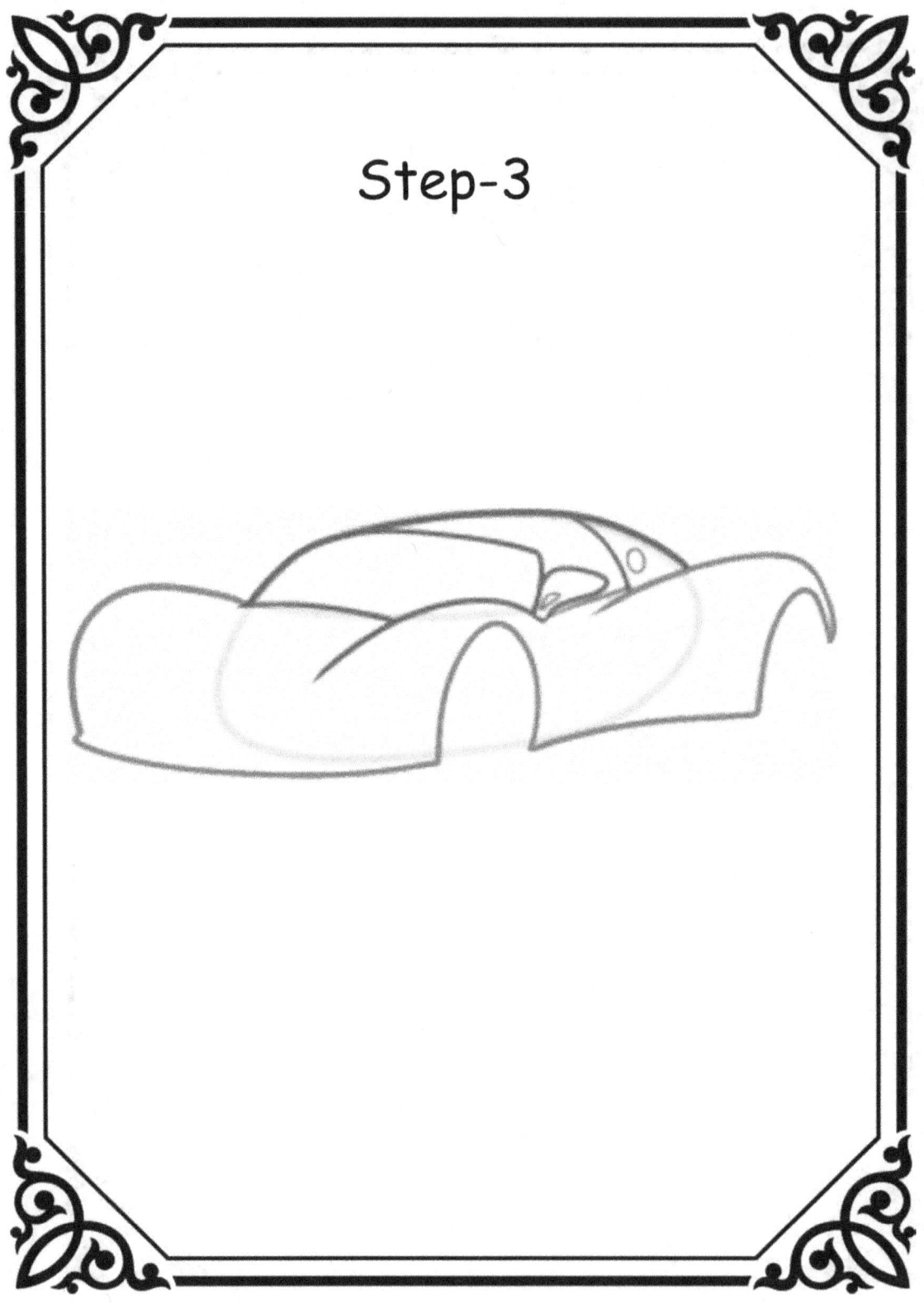

Step-4

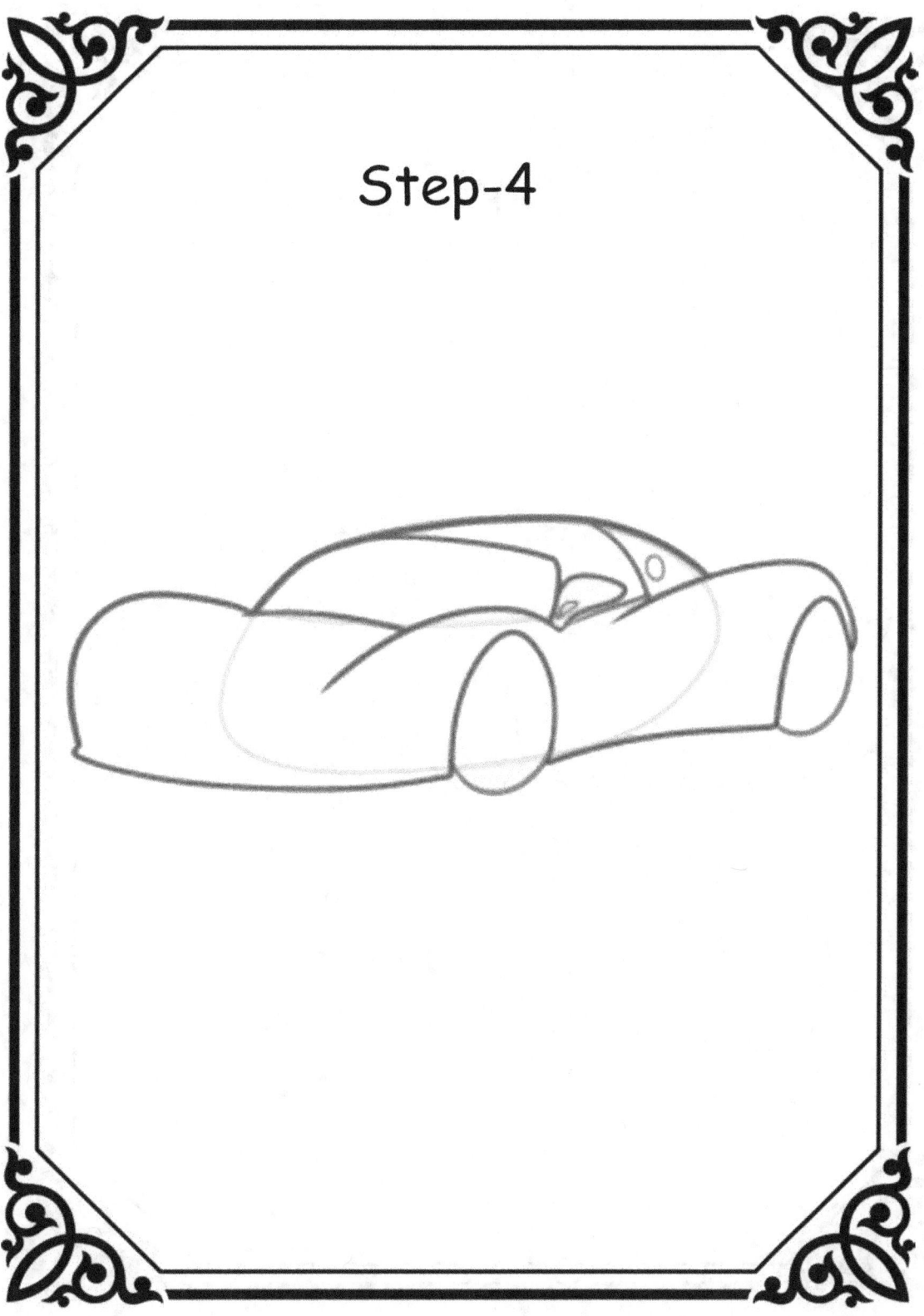

Step-5

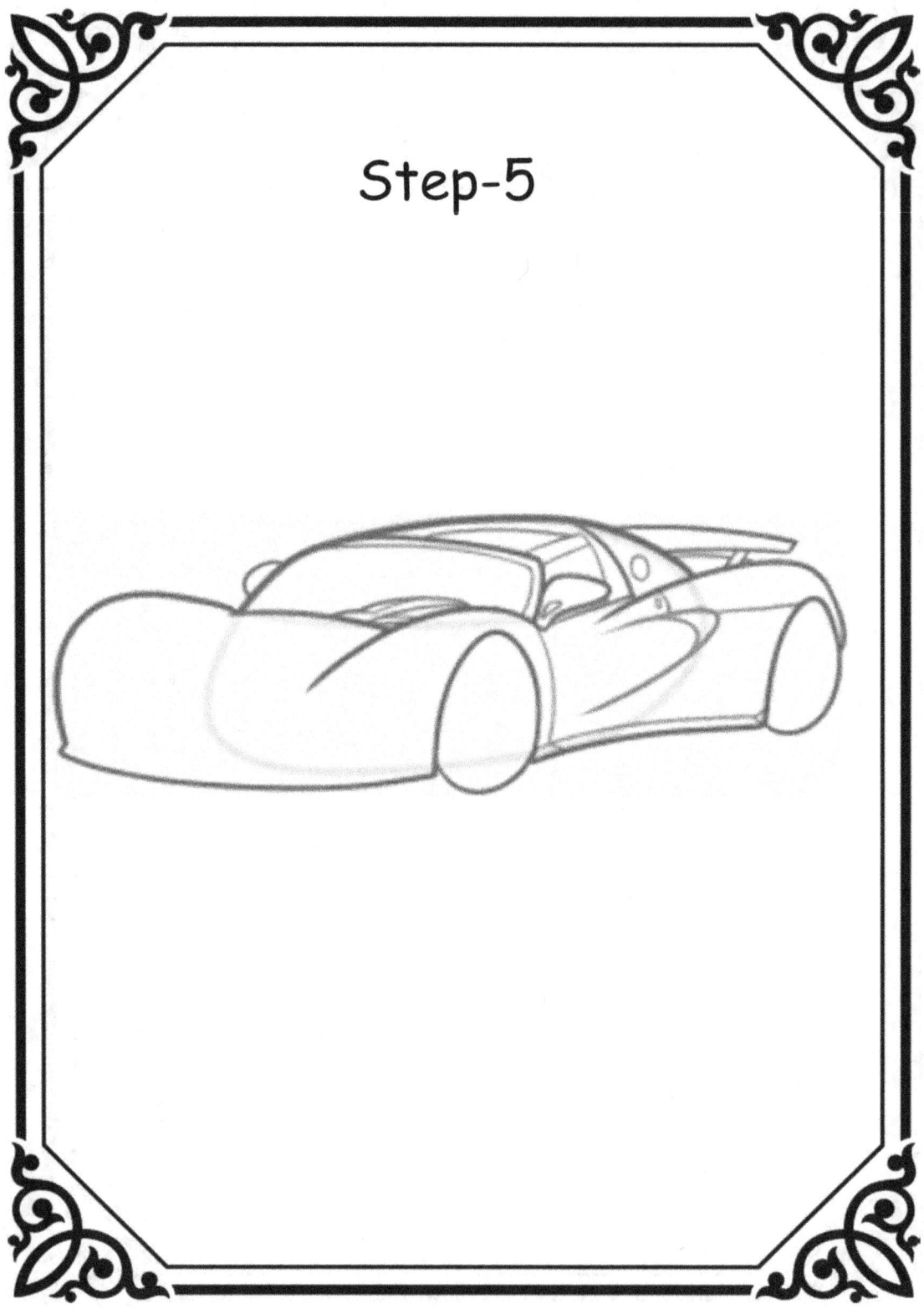

Step-6

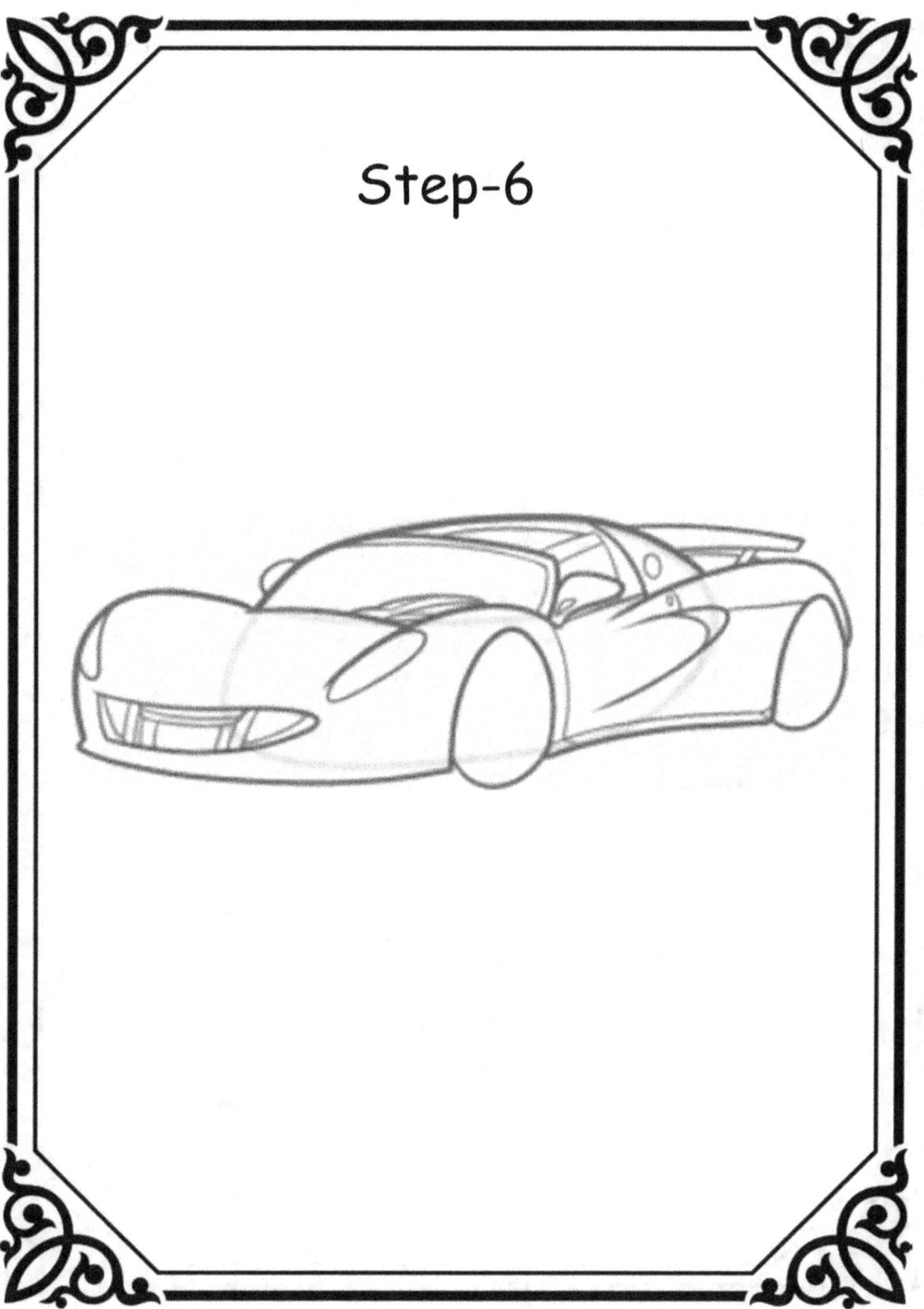

Step-7

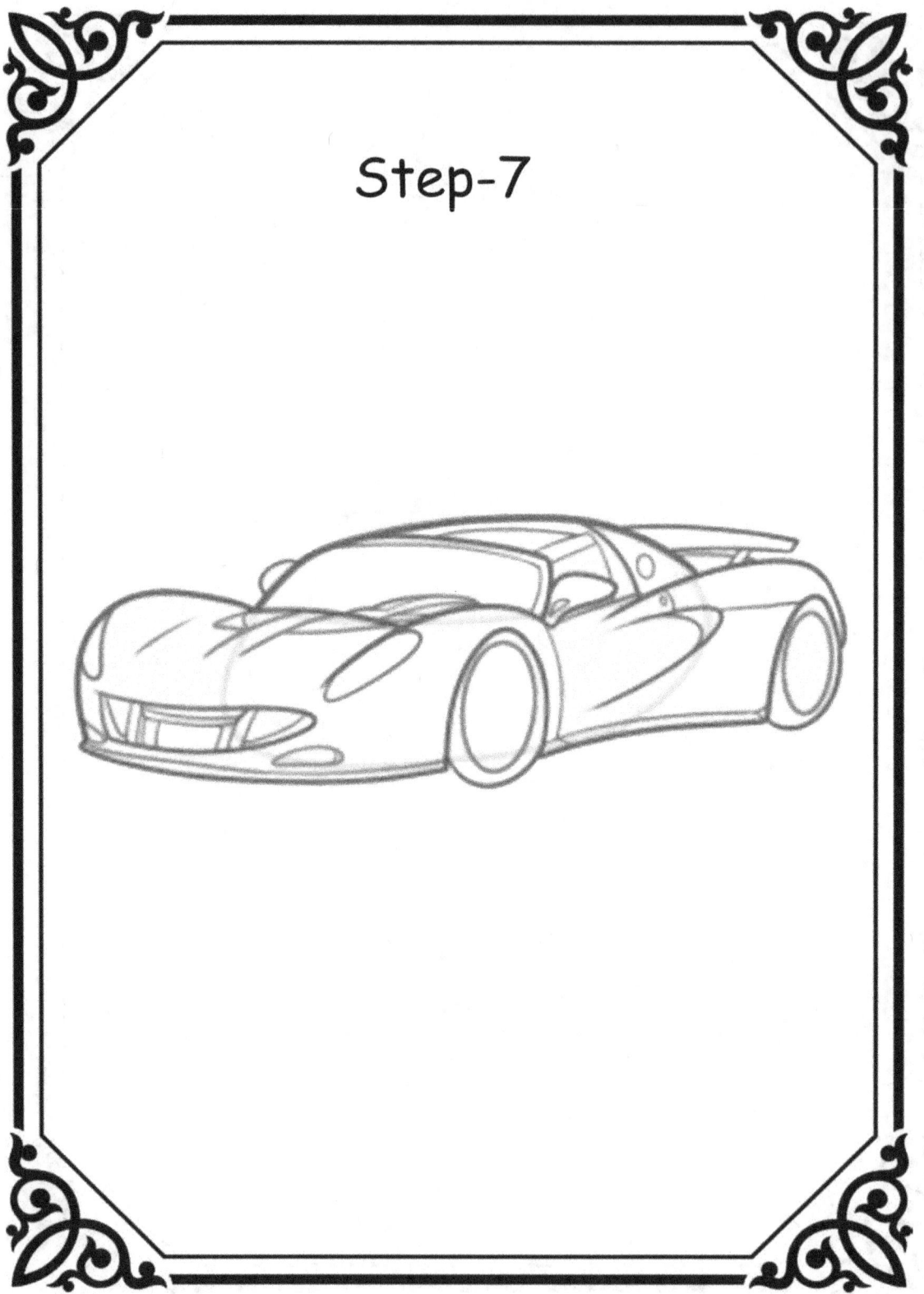

Step-8

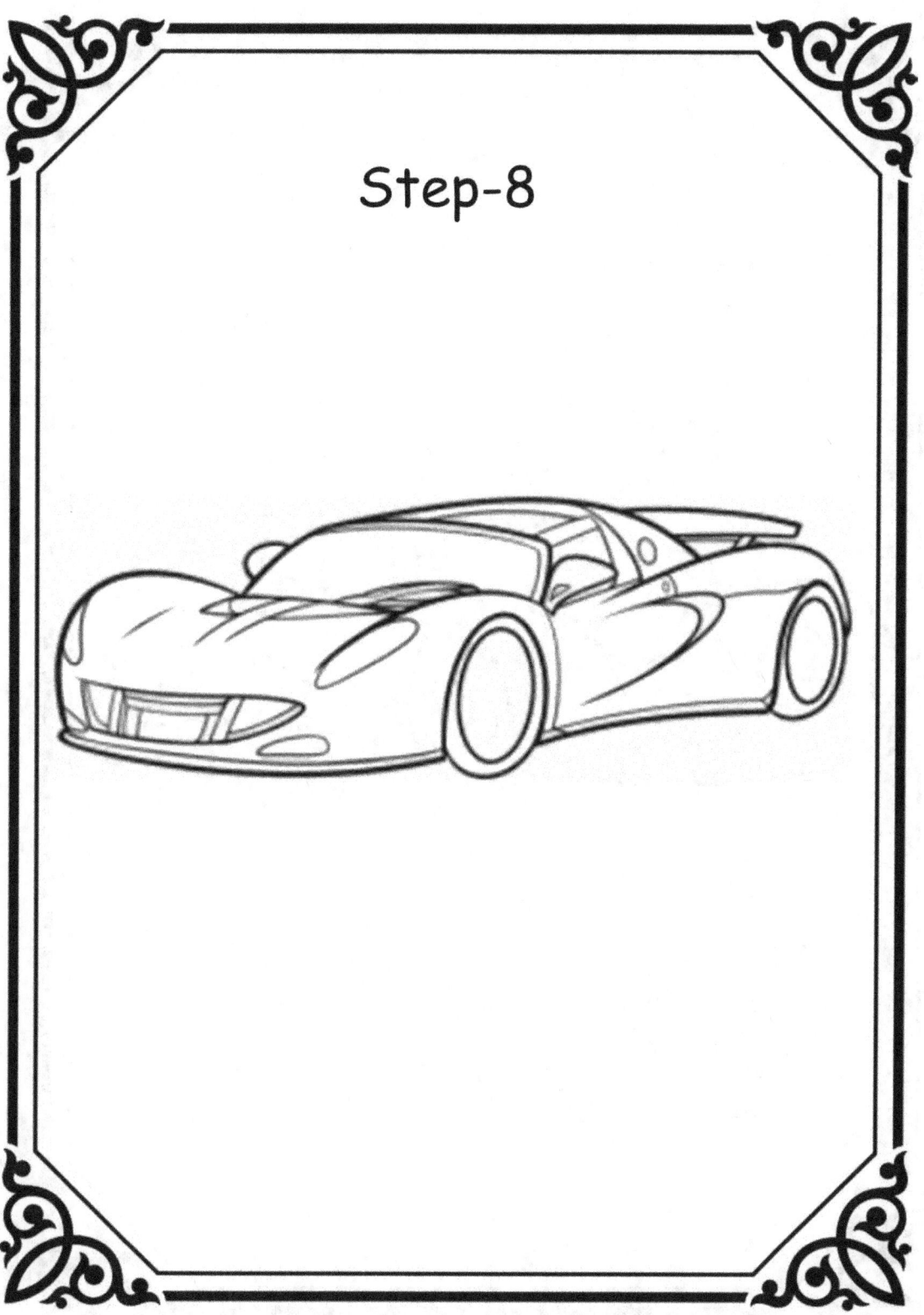

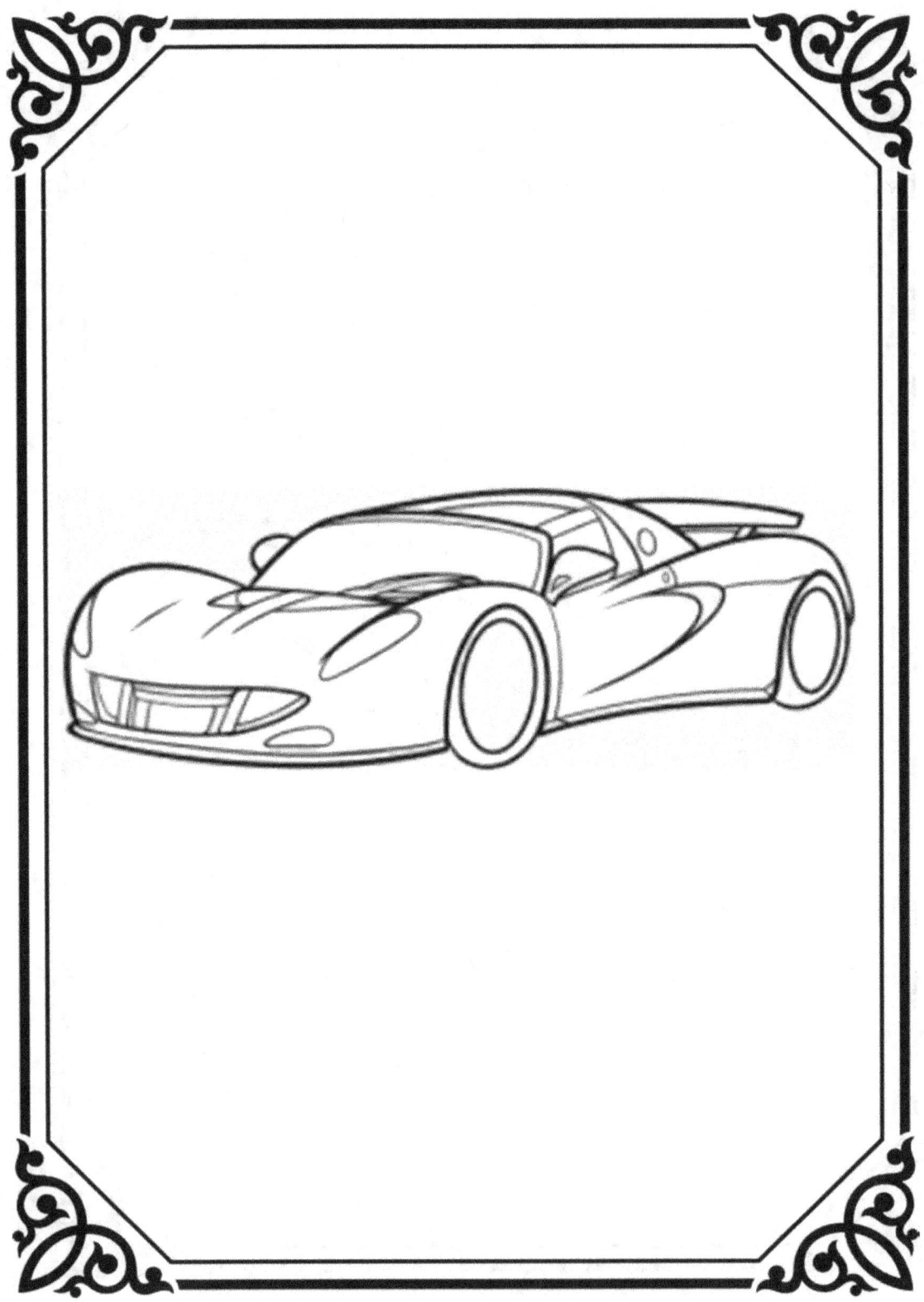

ALL RIGHTS RESERVED. No part of this publication may be reproduced or transmitted in any form whatsoever, electronic, or mechanical, including photocopying, recording, or by any informational storage or retrieval system without express written, dated and signed permission from the author.

DISCLAIMER AND/OR LEGAL NOTICES:

Every effort has been made to accurately represent this book and its potential. Results vary with every individual, and your results may or may not be different from those depicted. No promises, guarantees or warranties, whether stated or implied, have been made that you will produce any specific result from this book. Your efforts are individual and unique, and may vary from those shown. Your success depends on your efforts, background and motivation. The material in this publication is provided for educational and informational purposes only and is not intended as financial advice. The information contained in this book should not be used as an investment advice. Always consult a professional financial advisor before investing. Use of the programs, advice, and information contained in this book is at the sole choice and risk of the reader.

www.ingramcontent.com/pod-product-compliance
Lightning Source LLC
Chambersburg PA
CBHW081100240526

45465CB00025B/2775